ALL AT SEA

An Innocent Abroad

First Published in 2023
Published by M & H Books

Paperback ISBN: 978-1-7394954-0-4
eBook ISBN: 978-1-7394954-1-1

Cover Design and Book Layout by:
SpiffingCovers.com

Disclaimer
As memory fades with advancing years, please forgive any inaccuracies of sequence, dates or other details.

NB:i. All Biblical quotations are from the New International Version,(NIV) unless otherwise stated.
ii. All hymns quoted are in the public domain and not subject to copyright.

ALL AT SEA

An Innocent Abroad

Mike Gale

Initially I intended writing this book for my family, as a record of some of the many ways and blessings of God in my life. I am only too aware that, in the thick of it, the family was sometimes overlooked. Please forgive me. This is therefore primarily for my two adult children, Richard and Nicola, and my two grandsons, Tom and Will, growing up in a challenging world.

I would like to thank the following people:

My wife, Helen, for her love and support and the many hours spent at the computer, without which the book would never have been completed; David Cross, who encouraged me to write my story, gave up his valuable time to critique the first draft and also wrote the foreword; Rachel, whose friendship, help and computer skills so often saved the day and kept us sane in the process.

Mike in uniform of 3rd officer, aged nearly 21

Jesus, Savior, pilot me

Over life's tempestuous sea;

Unknown waves before me roll,

Hiding rocks and treach'rous shoal;

Chart and compass come from Thee;

Jesus, Savior, pilot me!

(Edward Hopper)

Contents

Foreword

Some years ago, when I first heard Michael telling a few of the stories of his extraordinary experiences in the Merchant Navy, I really hoped that he would have the opportunity to record them all in a book. And here it is!

Many of the tales recorded sound as if they come from life at sea centuries ago, but Michael was able to have adventures in the post-war maritime world of the 1950s and '60s that would not be possible or even permitted today. And what is so encouraging about all these amazing experiences is that he not only survived but he could see the hand of God on his life through all the ups and downs of the sometimes dark world in which he found himself. As God protected him and guided him, Michael was able to move from his time at sea into the fullness of his destiny in the Lord, bringing all that he had experienced into helping others in their journey of faith.

I wholeheartedly recommend this book to anyone who would like to read the story of this man's remarkable journey from boyhood to manhood in the company of his loving and faithful Heavenly Father.

David Cross
Ellel Ministries
June 2023.

Prologue
The Foundational Years

I should never have been born. My mother was told by doctors that she would no longer be able to conceive after the birth of my sister. So, I was a 'miracle' – a surprise, but wanted and loved. I believe my mother went into a private hospital without any finance to pay the fee, but a friend gave her the money, slipping the ten shilling note into a magazine.

Dad joined the RAF in 1939 when I was two years old. My sister Liz (who was eleven months older), Mum and I were left, like millions of others, to live as best as we could to survive the bombing of London and later on Doodlebugs and landmines. Our family doctor advised us to evacuate to Bramley in Yorkshire, which we did because of the detrimental effect it was all having on us. In particular, I was becoming a very nervous child. The sound of the wind blowing in the rigging of the barrage balloons was very scary, especially in the middle of the night. Although our stay there was brief, it was in Yorkshire that I learnt to sledge and spin a top, still wore short trousers and acquired chapped knees. Frozen school milk was another delight; it never quite thawed out in front of the classroom's open coal fire.

Sometime before this I had survived bronchitis, pneumonia and whooping cough. Dad was called back from the war as it was thought I might die. (I have recently found the original letter from the doctor requesting my father's immediate return, as it was feared I would not recover.) I then spent two separate spells in Friern Barnet Isolation Hospital (three weeks each time) with scarlet fever. Mum said she'd be back soon, but that was the last I saw of her for the next three weeks, and I remember wondering if she was coming back or had left me for good. Needless to say, I was not a strong lad, but I survived and enjoyed picking up shrapnel and collecting cigarette packets and matchboxes, like other kids.

After Yorkshire we returned home to our little flat in Finchley, North London. Dad was eventually demobbed, having served his final months in the RAF as part of the French Lorraine Squadron based in Douai, Northern France. I can remember the joy of his return, but also a certain amount of fear: I had hardly seen him for six years. What was he like? Our flat in East Finchley was small and I still have a great memory of Dad bathing me in a large galvanised tub. His hands were huge; it felt really good, and so for once a week I was clean!

Before the war Dad had been a skilled carpet-layer and planner, and on his return he and his brother set up a carpet-laying business together in Euston. My education suffered a bit as I tried to adjust between the different curriculums in London and Yorkshire, or maybe I simply wasn't too bright. Overall I went to five different schools. By all accounts I was a crazy kid, doing stuff which at times was dangerous; it seems I liked a dare. A few of us used to climb over the fence which guarded the electric tube train line, to put a penny on a rail and see how it became flattened as the train passed.

Then came a family holiday. Dad drove us all down to Dorset, to a guest house in Swanage – all four of us in one room, with starched white sheets as stiff as boards. When the National Young Life Campaign pitched a marquee in a field almost opposite, it was natural we would go. Mum and Dad were committed Christians, attending Highgate Tabernacle. Later I was to learn it was Irish Calvinist, which sadly imparted a very strict Christian lifestyle, leading to much false guilt in later years. Anyway, at the age of nine, I met with Jesus there in that tent and gave my life to Him. I'm told my mother came looking for me, asking folk if they had seen a small boy, wearing a blue shirt and trousers. She found me at the front of the marquee. I can still remember how real the Cross was to me – a large wooden one stood at the front of the marquee.

Soon after this, Mum had to go into hospital for a serious operation. My sister went to stay with an uncle and aunt, and I went to stay with my grandparents in Cheshunt, where Mum had grown up. Her four brothers were still living in the area. I was enrolled in a local primary school, where once again I felt completely lost. I think this led to me being a bit wild. My grandma used to give me a piece of bread covered in sugar, and I would climb a tree to enjoy the view and the treat. I loved my grandma so much, but Grandad had a very short temper. On more than one occasion he hit me really hard, even knocking me across the room, before sending me off to bed without a candle. I was scared of him, but there were good times, and after three months Mum and Dad arrived to take me home.

Life in East Finchley returned to normal, though ration books were still required, but that was normal for us anyway. On one occasion I can remember all the kids in the road coming out waving bananas – a real treat, as none of us had ever seen a real banana before! Life at school, church and the local Brethren Sunday School was resumed. However, memories of these days are painful. Yes, I mucked about but, looking back, I was very badly treated by one particular teacher and most Sundays, on my way home, I was bullied by some of the older boys. Once again, fear became part of my life, but I grew to enjoy Juco's (Junior Covenanters) and loved fretwork and the games. A Mr Small was the leader. He was small (!), kind and aided by the Markwick brothers, who had been medics in the Para Regiment. Brethren services were heavy going, but suddenly I discovered girls! I was so self-conscious, but at the same time was trying to understand what on earth was going on. Did I used to blush!

The young people's 'thing' in those days was called a 'squash', where as many as possible crowded into a room to hear the gospel and have a good time together. By now I was attending the Alder Secondary School, hadn't a clue where babies came from, loved roller-skating and got chucked out of the Cubs for setting off jumping crackers (uncontrollable fireworks) in the hall of the venue, East Finchley Baptist Church. In an effort to improve my education, Dad enrolled me at Clark's College, a private school, where I kept falling in love with one girl after another.

After being expelled from the Cubs, I joined the Sea Cadets. It was there that my interest in the sea took off, as we practised drills, learned seamanship and gunnery skills, and rowed on the Thames in a 27 foot naval whaler. I achieved leading seaman, obtained my quartermaster badge on *HMS Jamaica* – the first cruiser in action in the Korean War – and my gunnery badge at the Whale Island Gunnery School in Portsmouth. One Remembrance Sunday, I was a very proud part of the guard of honour at the North Finchley Remembrance

Memorial. Many years later, in the port of Bluff, New Zealand, I would join with the local servicemen in representing the Merchant Navy on Anzac Day.

Girls were the major reason for my leaving the Brethren Church to join Muswell Hill Baptist Church – there were more of them at Muswell Hill! By this time I had left Clark's College and joined the London Nautical School as a cadet, in training to become a Merchant Navy apprentice deck officer. I was fourteen and a half and travelled daily from my home in North London to Blackfriars: trolley bus to East Finchley Station, tube train to Waterloo and a walk down Stamford Street – an hour there and an hour back. It was at the time of the Festival of Britain. An air of excitement was abroad and, interestingly for me, my father was responsible for all the carpet planning and fitting at the brand new Royal Festival Hall.

It wouldn't be wrong to say we were a wild bunch at the nautical school but, of all the subjects on the curriculum, navigation and seamanship were top of the list. Rowing on the Thames was a firm favourite too, but very tough, taken by Captain Harvey, who had a voice just like a foghorn. We would start at Blackfriars Bridge and bust every gut to get to Waterloo Bridge against the tide. The 'foghorn' never stopped 'til at last we made it. Then, "Rest on your oars," was the longed-for command, *but* within five minutes the tide had swept us back to Blackfriars, and the boom of Captain Harvey's voice echoed across the water, "Give way together," and we had to row all the way back again!

English, too, was fun. We were studying *The Gun* by C. S. Forester and one of the lads, known as 'Hoppy', made a miniature brass cannon, with the intention of breaking into the stationery cupboard in our top floor form room. After several additions, like traces and a strong carriage, the cannon was ready. It so happened that November 5th was near and so bangers were readily available. Hoppy screwed down the traces on a desk, stuffed the mouth with lead shot (the lead having been obtained from the school roof) and applied gunpowder to the touch hole. Alas, Hoppy's tentative efforts were of no use, so Windy (my nickname) took over. The cannon exploded and the cupboard door shattered. The room filled with smoke and I was thrown backwards over the desks. Dazed, and with my face covered with black powder pock marks, I came round to see Captain Gibbs, the master, standing at the door with clenched fists. I escaped – fast.

The next morning Hoppy arrived at the school gates with a sheet of plywood. We never did get anything from the cupboard.

We also had a mad French teacher who always wore a black beret and a dirty raincoat. He had a habit of coming out with a particular statement – which to us as young adolescents seemed crazy: "The ugliest thing in the world is a nude woman." I had never seen a nude woman, not even half a nude woman. Well, it didn't work to put us off, for it was his room that provided the venue for covertly reading 'how to do it'!

Looking back, there are few negative feelings towards my mum and dad, but the lack of godly (or even any) sex education led to a lot of wounding as I grew up, not least when Dad walked out on the family for a while. By this time we were living in our own semi-detached house, not far from London's infamous North Circular Road. On this particular occasion I was the first one home and therefore the first to read the letter he had left for my sister and me, telling us he was leaving. Mum was expected home soon, on her return from visiting Grandad Coles, her father, who lived in Cheshunt. It fell to me to meet her at the bus stop, where I somehow found the courage to tell her that Dad had gone. He did eventually return. I can't remember how long he was away but he gave me a Christmas present – by post, I think – *The Wavy Navy*, signed *Daddy, 1951.*

My boyhood memories are sketchy, although I know Dad loved his time in the RAF then, after demob, his carpet trade went well, but for him it was 7 a.m. to 7 p.m., meaning I still saw little of him.

As time approached for us to leave school and take apprenticeships, we all calmed down. I was suspended for a few days for throwing lighted paper planes at the English teacher whilst he was writing on the blackboard with his back turned. Others were involved but only I owned up. I still had this deep sense of being a Christian, but how on earth did this work out in the environment of sea school?

At the church youth fellowship, we played handball every week in the hall, where the windows were protected with iron bars, but Saturday nights with the girls was the main attraction. Along with others I continued to fall in and out of love. The aura of sea school and its uniform probably gave me a certain glamour, and perhaps one of my crowning achievements was to be the number one target for the girls' Bible class leader, who made sure I wasn't anywhere around when 'her girls' emerged from class! It was 1952/53 and the burning question was 'How to live a Christian life?'. Every Sunday I recommitted my life to Jesus, promising not to swear or tell dirty jokes. My parents had no answers – the mention of sex or anything related was taboo. Monday morning brought about a total collapse of my sincere desire to follow Him with all I had. I was miserable. There were well over a hundred or maybe even two hundred in the very middle class youth fellowship, but I went to sea school, a very different place, and my peers were mostly at the secondary modern school.

I loved the young men's Bible class. There were twenty to thirty of us with Alan Fisher, the leader – a frail sort of chap, but gifted in making one feel wanted. To my surprise, he invited me to go to his home in Crouch End, North London, for tea. (The church was in Muswell Hill.) This was 1952 and at that time London was in the grip of what was to become one of its last great smogs. (For those who have never experienced smogs, these were a combination of industrial smoke, coal burning fires and fog, resulting in dense, impenetrable, yellow fogs, which were the cause of many deaths and much traffic chaos.) I had to walk home from school from the underground station – about one mile, no buses; men walked in front of vehicles with flaming torches to guide them. It was on one of these days that I had agreed to meet Alan Fisher; he wanted to have a chat with me. From home to the Crouch End clock tower where I was to meet Alan must have been four to five miles, a route unknown to me, but I had an inner conviction that I *had* to get there.

Most of the journey I made with my hand on hedges, hoping I'd make it to the other side of the road safely. The top of Muswell Hill was clear, but Crouch End lay at the bottom of a 1:10 hill and there the smog was very thick. Alan was waiting for me by the clock tower, and off we went to his home in Cecil Park Road, where this young man found a welcome and dainty cucumber sandwiches (oh dear!). So why the invitation? Apparently, I was proud!

Looking back, I think I still have a bit of the same problem of often playing up when unsure of myself and not wanting to look an idiot, not sure what to do. There was little conversation in our home, other than general chat such as "How was your day?" and Mum and Dad were fairly isolated. So now with Alan the real issue came out: how to live for Christ outside of church life. The answer? The Word of God. Alan took me through Chapters 6, 7 and 8 of the book of Romans and then to Galatians 2:20. I was to reckon myself indeed dead to sin and alive to God. Yes, like Paul in Chapter 7, I longed to do a lot of stuff, but couldn't and constantly fell. Backsliding was a big word in those days. Galatians 2 meant I died with Christ on the cross; ie my 'self-life' had died with him. In effect, I too had been nailed to the cross. 'No condemnation', says Romans 8; His Spirit lived *in* me. We knelt by the sofa. Precious moments passed as I experienced His power and forgiveness surging through me.

I walked home on cloud nine. Everything had changed. Temptations fled as I pronounced, "I am crucified with Christ, reckoning myself to be dead to sin and alive to God!"

I couldn't stop witnessing to my fellow school mates. I was banned from reading *The Christian Herald* (a popular Christian paper at that time) at break times in the science lab ("Windy's got religion!"); I spoke in the Open Air meetings. The time a friend and I went to 'witness' in the King's Cross area was hilarious. It was raining very hard, so I lifted up my voice outside a block of flats and preached about Noah. To our knowledge not a single window was open! But it was a love for the Bible that gripped me. I couldn't stop reading it and had to buy a torch so that I could read it under the bedclothes when Mum and Dad demanded I turn my light off. How clear is the memory of discovering Isaiah – so full of prophecy. My heart and my mind cried out, *Where are the prophets today?* I longed to be a prophet, but how? It was many years later that I received that very precious gift of prophecy. Looking back, I know I was baptised in the Holy Spirit whilst kneeling before God on that day, in Alan Fisher's house.

This brings me quickly to my baptism in water in September 1953. Four of us in the youth fellowship were baptised, and the hymn I chose for my baptism was *O Jesus I have promised to serve thee to the end.* I didn't like the tune, but I loved the words.

In a few days I was to join my first ship. Mum and Dad had managed to obtain a grant for some of my uniform and kit, and we signed my indentures (nothing to do with teeth!), which meant that, in effect, my Dad and I had signed away my life for the next four years. I now 'belonged' to the company *and* the ship's master. The company was Bank Line, and their responsibility was to look after me and feed me, to keep me from places of ill repute, and to instruct me in the arts of seamanship and navigation, which were the only two subjects I had passed at GCE O-level anyway.

Although it's a bit of a cliché, I want to say that I really was on fire for God, so I was somewhat taken aback when, on that wonderful Baptismal Sunday, one of the very elderly deacons came to me and, after saying the usual sort of things, said words that were to stay with me for the rest of my life: "You will be very disappointed with yourself, but don't give up."

This stunned me. I genuinely could not imagine letting God down. I tried to grasp what he was saying, but the words seemed to be from another world. How could I let God down? My heart's desire was to live for Jesus. I thanked Mr Ford, and probably made a joke of it, for although Jesus was so real to me, something deep within was buried, blocked out. I was already learning to cope by being the joker.

So, at the age of 16, Dad loaded me into the car, the aluminium trunk he'd bought into the boot, and we headed for Euston Station, from where the steam train took us to Cardiff Docks. I was now a junior apprentice, totally bewildered, clinging to Jesus, saying goodbye to all I had known up to that time, and all this for my first year's wage of £70!

I have written at some length about my amazing experience in the London smog and my Christian family and environment, not just because it is true, but also because, eventually, those words of Mr Ford came to pass as predicted.

And so to sea.

PART I

LIFE AT SEA

SS Sheilbank – My First Ship

Chapter 1
Out into the Big Wide World

All Bank Line ships' names ended with 'bank', and as I stood there on the Cardiff dockside, gazing up at the *SS Sheilbank* (formerly the *Empire Takoradi*), like all ships that have completed discharge and repairs, she didn't look very shipshape. I can remember going aboard with the third engineer with whom I'd shared a cab from the station. He was a cockney from South London, with hands that shook a bit, and I have a lasting impression of him offering to contribute to the cost of the taxi only to produce a pipe from every pocket, but no money! I was to learn that the shipping company paid all expenses. The good old days of porters to carry one's baggage still existed, and from then on I could travel home and return free of charge. Being the junior apprentice, third of three, meant I was truly at the bottom of the pile, but we had a reasonable cabin between us. 'Titch', the senior apprentice, was from Newcastle, and I hadn't a clue what he was saying until well on into the voyage.

I guess everything contributed to the feeling of being utterly lost. Sea school prepared one for the basics of life on a merchant ship, but as to the reality of life at sea – nothing. The ship's crew numbered seventy in total – half deck and half engine room – all lascars (Indian seamen), except the pock-marked Chinese carpenter (a result of smallpox) and the senior engine room man. Then came the master, chief, second and third officers, and the chief engineer plus his team of second, third and fourth engineers – all of whom were white British. Our destinations were to be determined by the fact that the *Sheilbank* was a coal-burner; distances steamed depended on our ability to take on board coal bunkers and sometimes some of the cargo space, as well as the boat deck, was sky high with coal.

My strong memory is of an overwhelming and endless weariness. As apprentices, 'turn-to' was 0700hrs. We were 'put on the shake' at 0645, when a 'boy' – at least sixty years of age and one of the lascar stewards assigned to us – would present us with tea and toast. Meals were breakfast at 0800, lunch 1200 to 1300, and dinner 1700 to 1800, and these were all served in the officers' dining room. 'Smokos' were fifteen minutes mid-morning and mid-afternoon. To begin with, work mainly entailed getting shipshape for the voyage across the Atlantic to Newport News, Virginia. We were to carry no cargo, as Bank Line had an agreement with other shipping companies not to trade from the UK. The Gulf of Mexico was a typical starting place.

It was heavy work for a very skinny and physically weak sixteen year old. In my early apprenticeship days, I would deliberately volunteer for the heavier manual work to build up my strength. During the ship's stay in Cardiff I managed a weekend home to Finchley, a visit to Cardiff City Football Club and visits to Captain Morgan and family, who were Christians. Captain Morgan was a Bristol Channel pilot and belonged to a Christian seamen's organisation called Living Links, a network of Christians all over the world who offered hospitality to seafarers in port. Some were ex seamen, others port officials and missionaries.

The Living Links' members' booklet contained names, addresses and telephone numbers of these contacts. Many were from the Brethren Church, known for their hospitality – so loving and warm-hearted. Once the ship was tied up alongside, a shore telephone would be connected. A call would usually result in an invitation to their home and, of course, a lift, although it could sometimes be quite an experience using public transport and, for a young, totally 'green' apprentice, often scary.

The organisation was founded by the Brethren commodore master of the Union Castle Line, and was to play a big part in my time at sea. In later years my wife and I were privileged to be part of this network, when we lived near Chatham Docks in Kent.

More of this later, but for the moment I can truthfully say that I believe the love and care of many of these 'shore links' over the following years was to prove a lifesaver to me. Sadly, I can remember little of Captain Morgan or his family, but they lived in Port Talbot, a bus ride away from Cardiff, and by the time I had arrived there and enjoyed home cooking by an open fire, I was usually asleep! Ten hour shifts, 0700 to 1700, meal breaks included – it was exhausting.

Getting used to living on a ship was confusing, but also informative. I could already tie knots and was now learning to paint, sweep up, wash my own clothes (in a bucket in the officers' galley). We all wore uniform and that too needed sorting. Uniform consisted of the traditional navy top and trousers, apprentice epaulettes, starched white collar with collar studs (plastic ones had yet to hit the market), black socks and shoes and an officer's hat with the company badge. I think I did quite a good job with the starched collar! Tropical uniform was white shorts and shirts, apprentice epaulettes and white socks. As for work gear, that was way ahead of the fashion styles most of the world is now wearing. Yes, we were definitely trend setters – denim top and jeans! These could be bought in the USA with very long trouser lengths which could then be then cut off to suit. I well remember boiling the trousers endlessly in a bucket on the galley, trying to get as much blue dye out of them as possible. Usually in the tropics, away from any need to dress up, we just wore shorts, shirt and flip-flops. Just think, I was wearing flip flops in the early fifties! However, despite conditions of weather and work, full uniform had to be worn in the officers' saloon.

September 1953 proved to be dark and cold, with constant rain and wind. One day, about three weeks after my arrival on board, news came in that we were to set sail for Newport News, USA on September 23rd. The day came and we had to catch the tide in the small hours. My allotted station for arriving and leaving port was in the wheelhouse – better there than fore or aft, letting go from shore and tug, as at least the covered wheelhouse offered some shelter from the atrocious weather. We exited the dock and made our way into the Bristol Channel, dropped off the pilot and began to chug along at 10 knots, belching out thick black smoke. My life at sea had begun. Little did I know at that time that on this my first trip, I would be away from the UK for seventeen months. A lot of growing up can take place in that time, but so can a lot of seasickness!

As a coal-burner, the funnel boat deck was piled high with coal. We left port as a 'light' ship – in other words we had no cargo, only coal bunkers for ballast and drinking water, as we headed for Newport News, USA in order to take on more coal bunkers to get us to Port Royal, Jamaica for more coal, then out to the Gulf of Mexico, New

Orleans, Mississippi for Port Sulphur, where we would load rock sulphur as our main cargo for New Plymouth, New Zealand, via the Panama Canal.

I was soon to discover that the *Sheilbank* was what was known as a 'stiff' ship, the opposite being described as 'tender'. To put this in layman's terms: she had been built bottom heavy, in order to counteract the extra weight of tanks loaded in the tween decks and on the main deck during the war. Basic ship stability demonstrated that the centre of gravity moves towards the weight; add on the ship's bunkers, water for drinking, and domestic use plus cargo, and you have created a significant pendulum. Over the next few months, just about every known swear word would be used to try and release the sheer misery of life on board in any conditions other than a flat calm. I was also soon to learn that there was a reason why all chairs in the saloon were secured to the deck and wooden covers fixed to the tables, which had individual holes for glasses, plates, knives, forks, etc. It was not uncommon for lifelines to be rigged, even when there was no storm, as seas and swells caused the *Sheilbank* to pitch and roll, making life on board difficult and hazardous. The ship had a peculiar, vicious roll and would go right over to almost 45 degrees, forcing us to walk down passageways on the bottom of the bulkhead, then, at 45 degrees a pause, that's it, get ready for the opposite movement – but no, the old girl would do one last lurch before shuddering to a halt. It was that last movement that would carry away anything not lashed down.

It wasn't long before seasickness took over. In those days no medication was on offer. Eating? Not a good idea! Fellow seamen are not known for sympathy, particularly as I took to my bunk, where I spent much of this, my first crossing. Homesickness was soon to follow. I can remember crying, longing to be home in a safe place instead of in the middle of the Atlantic. Over the years I learnt how to cope with the dreaded 'lurgy', although I always found myself fighting sickness initially on return to the ship from long stays in port or shore leave, before quickly recovering.

My first arrival on deck in an Atlantic storm was a bit different from a trip across the Channel. Mountainous waves appeared to be threatening our safety as we rolled, holding on for dear life, pitching into waves where the bow disappeared under the water, then a great shudder as the bow lifted clear out of the sea with tons of water racing down the foredeck and exiting in waterfalls out of the bulwarks, only to be repeated again and again.

Eventually we arrived in Newport News, USA. I'd been seasick for most of the journey. Our stay was unexpectedly prolonged, due to necessary repairs. Amongst other things, the *Sheilbank* was a rivetted ship and because of this the heavy seas caused her to 'hog and sag'. Let me try to explain: steel ships bend and a wave in mid-length will cause the bow and stern to drop a little. Suspended by a wave fore and aft, the middle part of the ship will sag. This, plus the impact of thousands of tons of water on the bow, causes the ship's plates at the bow to 'pant' – in other words they are pushed in and out, even though the bow, for obvious reasons, is the strongest part of the ship, being reinforced with cross beams and ribs much closer than those midships. Because of this 'panting', during the crossing of the Atlantic we sheared hundreds of rivets, hence the delay as we waited for the ship to be re-rivetted. It was hardly surprising that this, my introduction to life at sea, saw me sick and in my bunk for most of that time.

We may have been delayed but there was no shore leave whilst in Newport. I well remember going to the fo'c'sle to get a better look at the port and to take a photo. No sooner had I lifted the camera to my eyes than I heard the loud crackling of a loudspeaker and a voice boomed out *"No* photos in the dock!" So my first brush with the 'Yanks' and the way we were referred to as 'f***ing Limeys' wasn't exactly welcoming! A couple of days before arriving in 'the land of the free' we had to fill in a card declaring we were not communists, and our Chinese chippy was refused entry, as McCarthyism – a period of intense anti-communism activity in the States – was rife. What was even more unpleasant was the 'short-arm inspection': all of us had to have an army-style medical. I can still hear the rough command, "Okay, drop 'em!" I'm pretty sure I had no idea what venereal disease was, as the only naked woman I had ever seen was in a magazine.

The name of the next port – Port Royal, Jamaica – was exciting, the legendary place of pirates and Captain Morgan. The weather was now glorious – hot sunshine. October/November temperatures in northern latitudes were replaced by daytime heat previously unknown to me.

Loading coal is a dirty job. Scores of Jamaicans were covered head to foot and apprentices had a lot of cleaning up to do. Evening came. 1800hrs, pitch dark. No bunkering until morning. All the officers except the first mate and duty engineer had gone ashore for the first time since Cardiff four or five weeks earlier. We had a few US dollars left over from our stay in Newport, so 'Titch', the senior apprentice from Newcastle asked the first mate if we too could go ashore. Apparently a shop or bar was just up the road, not that we could see it as there were no lights and it was pitch black. The mate was very reluctant but finally gave in so off we went and thus began a remarkable experience of God's safekeeping.

I remember the darkness, for it was like a blanket over my head. I was aware that something was at the side of what was a rough pathway-cum-road. After about ten minutes we could see a light which gradually came into focus as some kind of café. For me it was very strange – obviously a place for drinking, but there were also women there... It felt very wrong and I felt very uneasy, especially when an old crone insisted on jumping up on my lap! What did I want to drink? "A coke." Soon afterwards an older man came in shaking a tin; he was collecting for the Salvation Army. Sensing this as my way out (lots of SOS prayers), I asked if he would take me to the Salvation Army. Strange looks all round, then 'Yes', he would. So out into the darkness we went. I had already said I was a Christian and the reality and sense of trusting God was immense. My rescuer led the way and, as figures emerged from the darkness, he kept calling out again and again, "Christian, Christian," until they melted away. I remember the hill up which we climbed led to a large lit house where we were welcomed and which turned out to be the home of a Seventh Day Adventist who was in the middle of packing his bags prior to flying back to Florida. After a chat I was asked if I had any US dollars – only a few, but this was the guarantee that my escort would return me safely to the ship. So once again out into the pitch dark and a guaranteed safe journey, but of course Father God was protecting me every inch of the way. Phew – the naïve sixteen year old was learning fast!

Loading bunkers continued the next day. The ship had what is called a 'Smoke Room' – supposed to be a kind of lounge – where a very old shortwave radio occupied one corner. With patience and hope I tried to get a station. I don't know if you can imagine what it was like at that moment to hear an old gospel song coming from the radio, *It Is No Secret (What God Can Do) written by Stuart Hamblen and sung by Elvis Presley and Jim Reeves, amongst others*.

Yes, seems He had kept and protected me on my way out of what was a brothel (what on earth was a brothel anyway?) and back to safety. As I listened, a black face, even more blackened by coal dust, appeared at the porthole. "Me too Christian," he said, and out of his shirt pocket he pulled a New Testament. "This my sword," he said. I'll never forget the incredible smile filling his face, white teeth gleaming and joy pouring out of his eyes. My fellow traveller had to go and continue shovelling coal for bunkers, and not long afterwards we sailed for New Orleans. This was the first Christian I had met since leaving Cardiff, and one of the very few I encountered on a ship during my eleven years at sea.

What followed would never be forgotten. Our first port of call was up the Mississippi to load sulphur rock – probably 8000 tons, at Port Sulphur, then back to New Orleans to load JCBs, four or five cars, huge cases of farm machinery plus two passengers, but it would take two to three days from Port Royal to New Orleans. The first mate decided to give us – the three apprentices – a 'job and finish'. At sea, it was normal to work through Saturdays and Sundays and often to work an extra four hours on top of the standard eight, so an eighty-four hour week was not unusual. Yes, it was tough, but I told myself I was building muscle! This 'job' turned out to be making sure the timber 'limber boards' which formed the bottom of the cargo holds on either side, covering the bilges, were tight. If any rock dust cargo found its way into the bilges, this would cause a blockage should the need arise to pump out water.

It turned out to be a nightmare. We started off using oakum to fill the gaps. When that ran out, sand and cement. When the sand ran out, clinker from the boilers. It must have taken us two or three days, but by the time we had finished our fingertips were absolutely raw. (Gloves? What gloves?) The sulphur was then loaded, using cranes and grabs, and as for the American stevedores, unlike us, they all wore protective clothing, including breathing apparatus. As apprentices, our job was to go below into the 'tween deck' and sweep up spillage. (The tween decks were for other cargo.) If a grab hit the hatch coaming causing a spark, as happened on a number of occasions, the sulphur dust ignited, with the potential to cause a fire. We then had to do a mad scramble up the ladder on to the main deck, holding our breath. Well, we survived. In 1953 apprentices were slave labour and Health and Safety was unheard of, except as far as all running gear on ships, such as derricks, rigging, blocks etc., which all had safe working load regulations; it was the humans who didn't. When it came to putting our fingers in water to wash, it was agony. It took quite a while for the sores to heal and our red eyes to recover from sulphur dust. Apprentice officers had to carry out every task that they would later order a crew member to undertake, fair, but at times painful!

I must have had some time off following this. It was raining. I had learnt from a local of a café about a mile up the road, so off I went, only to quickly discover that Americans – at least in that part of the country – didn't walk anywhere, especially if it was raining. Car after car slowed and pulled in, their occupants staring at me as if I came from another planet. The café was scary. Imagine a thin, scruffy 'Limey' approaching the bar and asking, in my very best English, for, "A Coca-Cola, please."

I was met with blank faces and, after I had tried several times and was feeling desperately embarrassed, a lady suddenly burst out, "Oh, ya mean a coke!" Then came my next shock as a policeman came in, took off his gun belt and laid it on the table. A gun? I had never seen a gun in my life, other than the remains of the 303s proudly displayed by the Sea Cadets. Well, I escaped and arrived back on board, shortly to sail for New Orleans.

Now that was some place! The famous Canal Street was a must to visit in New Orleans; jazz seemed to burst out of every café and bar. Sunday came and the three apprentices were given the day off. I decided to try and find a church and the other two agreed to come with me. Someone on the bus directed us to the First American Baptist Church and my re-education, this time in terms of what was 'church', continued.

A huge glass-fronted tank like a large aquarium took up the front wall of the auditorium. There was a baptism taking place: ladies and young children clothed in white dresses, skirts all weighted down (although it did take a few seconds for the hems to drop completely!), arms and legs thrashing about in the water. Afterwards there was the youth meeting – noisy, and the best part was meeting with some young nurses, who invited us out to swim in a nearby freshwater lake. It was great fun. One from Tennessee was incredulous (in a wonderful southern drawl): "D'ya really call a sidewalk a pavement?"; "How can ya have such little cars in England?"; "Wouldn't you boys look lurvly in a crew cut?"; "Ah think you English boys are just lurvly!" Being so upfront took a bit of getting used to, but having the attention of three gorgeous southern nurses certainly stirred the blood. However, as so often happened at sea, the time soon came to return to the ship. Being a Christian in that church looked to be very exciting. The English reserve was challenged in a number of ways, and so began yet another journey, discovering what it meant to be a Christian in another country – no pews, massive baptismal tank, girls who were outspoken and said what they thought. My Baptist/Brethren upbringing was beginning to look very dull, besides which, these girls wore short skirts and lipstick *and* played tennis on Sundays – a total 'no no' in many UK churches at that time.

In New Orleans we finished loading Caterpillar machinery, four American cars, some in crates, and then, to our surprise, two passengers – a married couple. Our port for discharge was New Plymouth, New Zealand, via the Panama Canal. If the weather and the old coal-burning tramp ship allowed, we could get there just before Christmas. It took almost six weeks. Little did I know that the following Christmas I would find myself in Buenos Aires, still on the same trip and still not having returned home. But first, the Panama Canal.

We arrived on the Atlantic side at night. The canal is the link between the Atlantic and Pacific Oceans and without it, the only alternative would be the long and dangerous trip around Cape Horn. I have memories of steaming through the freshwater lakes, where many ships pumped out and exchanged stale water for fresh. It was vital to be aware of the draught of one's ship, as a ship will be lower in fresh water than in salt water. The Plimsoll line has saved many lives, preventing captains from overloading, whether intentionally or unintentionally.

It was a beautiful night as we entered the canal. Three locks enabled ships to rise to the higher level of the lakes and then lower to the waters of the Pacific. The pilot slowly nudged us into the first lock and the adventure began… Motorised 'mules', attached either side by steel wires, moved along the lock on rack and pinion rails. Imagine a tropical night in Panama, with palm trees and lush vegetation, stars piercing the inky sky and, against this backdrop, the sound of the blues played on a large harmonica by one of the mule crew. It gave me goosebumps. And so it was until we cleared the locks and the Pacific side port of Balboa, and began what seemed to me to be the longest journey of my life – six weeks across the Pacific to New Plymouth, North Island, New Zealand.

Chapter 2
The Land of the Long White Cloud & Down Under

Many people ask, "What on earth do you do on a ship at sea?" Every day one wakes up, scans the sea looking for land. Nothing! At first it was a great adventure, but being with the same crew mates for almost six weeks without a break did cause a bit of friction.

A first year apprentice got all the dirty jobs such as cleaning out water tanks which serviced the officers' washrooms and which were not much bigger than the domestic water tank normally found in a loft. I had to climb through the manhole on the top and cement wash the inside. Constantly 'holy stoning' the master's deck was another rotten task; on our knees, we had to scour and clean the decks using a large block of whitening 'stone' with two hands, back and forth. It didn't help when I knocked over a pot of white paint. Hours of my 'time off' (no such thing at sea) were spent under the watchful eye of Captain Williams who, early on in the voyage, had sent me to fetch something from the 'fog locker' down aft. Eventually, after a lot of mickey-taking, I discovered there was no such thing as a fog locker! Steam winches operated the ship's derricks in port and a lot of grease and muck built up underneath these, so underneath I was sent with a sort of trowel to clean them. And then there was chipping… Any steel ship rusts. Hours and hours were spent with crew, chipping off the rust and then of course repainting. In good weather, getting rid of salt deposits from the superstructures was a priority. A wicked soda mixture was used – a pinch of caustic soda with some sort of soap – which was known to all as 'soogi' – don't ask me why! Then there was polishing brass, plus keeping yourself and your shared cabin clean and tidy. Clothes were hung out in good weather as they became quite damp, especially after a storm, despite being stowed in your cabin.

There was also the studying: my indentures, signed jointly by my father, the shipping company and me, stated that I would be 'taught all matters of seamanship and navigation'. So, from time to time I tried to study. Usually the second mate had a go at teaching us, the three apprentices. Then there was the thrill of learning to steer. Of course there was no gyro compass, just two magnetic ones – one in the wheelhouse and one on the monkey island, a small deck above the wheelhouse. The latter was also used for taking bearings of landmarks and the sun when it was on the horizon (known as amplitudes).

I always seemed to be ravenous. Ships were sometimes known as 'hungry' or 'okay'. (Hogarths, a shipping company, was always known as 'Hungry Hogarths'.) This being an Indian crew ship, I would wolf down the European meal followed by an Indian curry and any afters on offer, then back on deck and aft to the crew's galley to beg for any spare chapatis!

Needless to say, I was pretty tired most of the time. Bad weather on the *Sheilbank* was demanding and alarming; she was so stiff, as previously explained. My seasickness was less by now, but the strength required to cope with the storms added to the overall weariness. A skinny sixteen year old was learning how to survive.

We nearly always worked on Saturdays and Sundays. Ships don't stop for weekends. In poor weather, or simply as part of our training, we were put on watches: 8-12, 2-4, 4-8. If you were lucky to be on the 8-12 watch you would be on the bridge from 0800 to 1200, but after lunch would be working on deck with the crew for another four hours, then stood down until the evening meal, after which back on watch at 2000. That worked out to be a twelve hour day, which I think could justifiably be termed 'slave labour'. Try to imagine what it was like to be up again at midnight until 0400, then up again for breakfast at 0800, and working on deck until going on watch again at midday.

A great job was helping the third mate to inspect the lifeboats. All the safety equipment had to be checked: refill the water tanks; put up the sails if the weather permitted; check the lifeboat supplies – first aid equipment and especially the biscuits for weevils, then the davits and the falls (block and tackle used for lowering and raising the lifeboats). What always seemed to be a lost cause was to start the motor lifeboat engine, as it rarely worked.

To pass exams, all apprentice officers were also obliged to become familiar with the ship's engine – a massive steam triple expansion engine. Just imagine the extreme heat generated by the coal-fired boilers. Indian firemen (stokers) kept the boilers fired up, consuming bucketfuls of oats and water to help them avoid dehydration and keep going. I was friendly with John Brown, the third engineer from London, who would come up on deck from time to time. His way of keeping up the steam pressure was to turn off the cooling fans, resulting in engine room stokers flaked out on deck, gasping, "Oh, Sahib – no-ish steam, Sahib." (In those days Indian crews didn't understand the workings of electricity and for them everything was 'steam', so even if a bulb went they would solemnly declare, "Sahib, no-ish steam," which always made me laugh.)

As I've said, even as apprentices we were always woken for deck duties by an Indian steward bearing tea and toast. We really gave this chap a hard time by rudely teasing him about his beard and different culture. In 1953 one could get away with what would now be understood to be totally unacceptable. Sealife banter was a bit rough at times, but this chap was at least sixty years old and took it all in his stride; this was life at sea – no quarter given. This is just how it was. No such thing as being off sick either; you worked until you dropped. Never mind if, in the tropics, temperatures below decks and in the accommodation were over 100 degrees Fahrenheit.

Inevitably, I became homesick from time to time. I clearly remember, on a few occasions, missing my mother so much and crying myself to sleep. And then there was the Pacific: would it never end? If allowed into the chart room, one could see where the ship was – only another inch along the course! Let's face it, we did well to make 10 knots – an amazing 240 miles a day. As mentioned before, relationships became strained; officers no longer seemed to be friendly and the work became so boring, but a ship's library helped. I can remember reading some amazing books – if only I could remember some of the titles.

Then one day a particularly vicious storm arose. We were woken by a nerve-jarring screech. A couple of the heavy Caterpillar farm machines were on the verge of breaking free, and crew had the dangerous task of going below into the tween decks to re-secure the machines. On that occasion no one was injured, but it was very dangerous, as you can imagine. Then there were the passengers who couldn't wait for New Zealand to appear on the horizon. It was amazing when we finally looked at the horizon and saw land – grey lumps of land, mountainous, rising higher and higher as we steamed nearer. However, the sea was to give our passengers a memorable farewell. A big storm in the Southern Ocean produced a huge swell, throwing all of us out of our bunks. We tried sleeping on the cabin floor. The 'boy' (steward) had left a number of buckets filled with water in an anteroom off the saloon, and we arrived to find the water and buckets sloshing and charging all over the deck as the ship rolled from side to side. The passengers were terrified, whereas we apprentices just laughed and laughed, but all the time hanging onto anything we could get hold of. I must have begun to get my sea legs.

At last New Plymouth – a very beautiful part of the North Island. We tied up alongside what was then the only wharf – a wooden one – using our lines, but also massive hawsers from the wharf, in recognition of the Southern Ocean rollers which could tear a ship from her lines. Mount Egmont, capped with snow, the second most perfect volcano cone in the world, dominated the small town. As usual, when reaching land after a lengthy period at sea, it took a while for us to stop swaying and stumbling around, but all tensions and supposed insults etc. vanished, as we had at long last achieved a major part of our voyage.

As a Christian I was isolated. All the officers and the other apprentices knew I was a Christian. I had shared my faith and didn't swear, but I was very naïve, not yet having experienced some of the despotic behaviour and places of deprivation. Stepping on to the wharf with one of the apprentices, I discovered a Seamen's Mission. A very large lady in charge quickly told us that the people she felt most sorry for in all the Merchant Navy were Bank Line apprentices. She knew how hard we had to work. "Tea and cakes?" Heaven! "What would you like to do?" she asked.

"I'm a Christian," I replied. "I want to go to church." At once she told me of a Baptist church nearby, grabbed a phone, and arranged for me to meet a chap the very next day.

I soon got to know Bill Marsden from the church and can remember his address to this day: 144 Powderham Street, New

Plymouth, N.Z. In a few days' time it would be Christmas. Christmas 1953 in the glorious southern hemisphere – hot, exciting, different – would leave me with many wonderful memories. Father God was looking after me as always. How faithful He is: 'I will not fail you or forsake you' (Joshua 1:5, NASB). And so began a new, fresh experience of what it was to be a Christian in New Zealand.

The master, somewhat reluctantly, allowed me shore leave over the Christmas period. I stayed at Bill's and was quickly introduced to a number of young people from the church, one of whom lived in quite a large bungalow with a good-sized garden, which made a particularly lasting impression on me. By the time I had dug up a Christmas tree, picked some lemons and met Joan Anderson, whose uncle was the Lord Provost of Edinburgh, I was hooked. She was a few years older than me and became a real friend. Christmas, the magic of Mount Egmont and glow-worms in Pukekura Park were all the ingredients for a massive crush. Years later she married the owner of the largest bakery on the South Island (Invercargill), had two lovely young daughters and lived in a very modern bungalow with underfloor heating, hydro-electric power being very cheap, due to the Southern Alps.

For those of you who think seamen just travel around breaking girls' hearts ('a girl in every port'), let me tell you the opposite can also be true. When the ship left port I can remember shedding a few tears, as I sat in one of the heads (loos), feeling very alone. A small white handkerchief bearing her scent was all I had to remind me of Joan. In those days, a possible way to a young lady's heart wasn't just a uniform, but Old Spice aftershave. This sure was a hit in New Zealand in 1953/54, perfume being in short supply.

Whilst ashore, one of Bill's friends gave me the use of a car for a day, a small Fiat, although I'm pretty sure I didn't have a driving licence. He also offered me an opportunity to invest £1000 in his embryonic Mothercare-type business. Healthcare was all the rage in New Zealand then, as many of the postage stamps indicated, bearing pictures of children. It was, of course, impossible, as I was only earning the amazing sum of £5 12s 6p a month. Going ashore with a couple of pounds in my pocket made me feel like a lord, but any glimpse into a shop window soon brought me down to earth. Anyway,

I managed to drive the car some way up the dirt track on Mount Egmont – quite an experience, because a 4-track would have been more appropriate. New Zealand was a poor country then: most of the cars were old and secondhand, and young enthusiasts would hot rod the old Fords. Morris Minors were common – old side valve versions – and the speed limit was 50 miles per hour, but if you had foreign currency and you paid in currency other than New Zealand pounds, you could afford to import and be the envy of friends and everyone else. When I returned a few years later, Joan and husband Alec were the proud owners of a Mercedes. Baking bread must have paid well! Anyway, it was exciting being driven back from Invercargill to Bluff in a Merc instead of the bus, but that was a later trip.

(I'm writing this in full, because my first impressions and memories of New Plymouth were long-lasting. In 2003 my wife, Helen, and I visited New Plymouth at Easter, almost fifty years since my first call. 144 Powderham St, Bill's home, was still there, though no Marsdens, and the town had hardly changed, albeit the waterfront had been somewhat extended from the single wharf of 1953. Sadly, the Mission had gone; Egmont was now Mount Taranaki, Maori names having been restored, but the romance would never change or be lost.)

Our fourth engineer was a real character – a Scot who, on arrival, hit the bottle and spent many an hour sitting outside his cabin singing, "There was a wild colonial boy, Jack Duggan was his name." My non-conformist upbringing had not introduced me to any alcoholics, and anyway, alcohol was not allowed whilst the ship was at sea. This Scot was determined to spend Christmas in jail ("Food's better!"). Moored ahead of us was a small working sailing boat, and a very drunk fourth engineer decided he was going aboard. Word got around quickly and one of the wharfies told us to watch out; if one foot were to be put on board, drunk or uninvited, the intruder would be thrown off. Sure enough, soon the fourth mate's body flew through the air, landing in a heap on the wharf. I guess being drunk had some benefits, as it wasn't long before he picked himself up and staggered back onboard, seemingly unhurt.

Celebrating Christmas in New Plymouth was so very different: outdoor parties; barbecues on the beach; beautiful clear skies;

moonlight shining on Mount Egmont; almost like another world. Glorious sunshine certainly took the edge off being so far from home, but leave we had to, as sadly it was once again time to move on to our next destination, Geelong, Port Phillip Bay, Australia, where we were to be fitted with shifting boards in order to load grain for India. These timber boards were used to construct temporary compartments to prevent grain shifting with the ship's movement, with potentially disastrous consequences, such as the ship becoming unstable and more than likely turning over and sinking.

Our journey across the Tasman Sea was uneventful until we reached the Bass Strait, that relatively narrow stretch of water between Australia's Victoria Coast and Tasmania.

Any chart will show the Bass Strait to have an average depth of 50 metres. Strong northerly currents off the Victoria coast are often caused by strong, opposing southerly winds. This, plus tidal flow and the shallow waters frequently produces huge waves. Because of the deteriorating weather, the first mate put the apprentices as extras on all three watches. I was with the second mate on the 12-4 watch. The southerly wind, with nothing to check it from the South Pacific Ocean, combined with the shallow depth, was very dangerous. My outstanding memory was hanging on for dear life as 10,000 tons of light ship (no cargo) came crashing down, literally screaming off the top of a giant wave, without time to complete the pitch by coming back up. She just stayed down as another wall of water broke over the foredeck. Helpless, we watched in awe as water covered the fo'c'sle and mast houses, seeming close enough to touch as it climbed the accommodation almost to bridge height. The ship stopped and began to shudder. Gradually the bow rose and hundreds of tons of water rushed through the bulwark ports. How we eventually rose above the sea for yet another but lesser pitch, and how we survived, I'll never know, except that we were 'light' and therefore with masses of buoyancy. Fully loaded would have seen us dive straight to the bottom. Over the years many ships, large and small, have come to grief and been lost in the Bass Strait. For this, still my first trip to sea, it was all very scary, and both I and the second mate who was with me (a Scot with big black beard, blazing eyes and wild looking) knew we had come close to death that afternoon.

Sitting here in my study, sixty-five years later, I have a deep sense of the keeping power of a Mighty Saviour who, with a word, stilled the storm on Lake Galilee. It was Oswald Chambers who, some years ago, wrote a phrase which has stuck with me over the years: 'God sanctifies memory'.[1] Can you look back and see the hand of God in your life?

The *Sheilbank*'s engine and boilers needed repairs, which necessitated the shutting down of engine and auxillaries, meaning no hot water etc. This was to last three months and we made our way, courtesy of a Melbourne pilot, up the River Yarra and tied up to Spencer Street Wharf, Spencer Street being the city of Melbourne's famous railway station. Melbourne can get quite cold in the winter months and a steel ship with no heating is a little unpleasant, but I was an apprentice and apprentices have to learn not only to paint, but also to paint the draught numbers, ship's name and any company flag on the bows, and, of course, the Plimsoll line. So, over the side I went on a bosun's chair, almost to the water line. I didn't, however, reckon on the crazy second mate who took great delight in discharging his toilet over me, before appearing over the bulwarks, shouting and screaming with laughter. To him apprentices were *****. Here you'll have to fill in your own language! Fortunately, he was soon to be replaced, having decided, whilst very drunk, to climb up on to an old boiler in the dock and launch into a Highland fling, in the course of which he broke his leg. His replacement was a tall Aussie second mate – tough, but also more human.

Melbourne was a great place for a young man to discover: a large city, in Australian terms, with green trams and mad taxi drivers who joined in some of the punch-ups between customers as they fought over taxis. It was great walking down Colin Street – the buzz of people and shops so very different from that long 'steam' across the Pacific. Best of all, I had a contact in Melbourne.

Andrew Biggs lived with his parents in the suburb of Sunshine. He had belonged to the young men's prayer group set up in the early 1950s by the Reverend Alan Fisher when he was assistant pastor-

1 *Not Knowing Whither: The Steps of Abraham's Faith : a Series of Studies in the Life of Abraham*. Oswald Chambers. Oswald Chambers Publications Association. 1934, p12.

cum-youth leader at Muswell Hill Baptist Church, North London (he of the previously mentioned Crouch End Clock Tower and cucumber sandwiches fame). Andrew had since emigrated to Australia with his mother and father, a butcher by trade and also a Baptist minister; the older brother, John, was already in Australia.

One Sunday I made my way to Spencer Street Station and boarded the train for Sunshine. Footscray was a stop on the way – always remembered for the stench of the abattoir. My next surprise was when getting on the bus. Other than the driver, I was the only one on the bus who spoke English; all were *new* Australians – Hungarians, Greeks and many other Europeans.

The Biggs' home was a typical bungalow for that time – small, but oh what a welcome! After the church service it was home for some great Aussie tucker, but not before I spilt a cup of hot coffee all over the new lounge carpet – ouch! I was to visit this home many times. John had a car, and on the weekends when I visited he would decide on a night drive south through the Dandenongs towards Wilson's Promenade. His real interest was a lovely young lady, daughter of a fruit farmer in North Nar Nar Goon (wonderful names!). She had a sister. Both were too old for me, but I stayed there for a weekend and can still see their father's face when these two voluptuous young ladies came into the dining room; he was laughing at me, at the obvious, rapturous appreciation on the face of a poor apprentice miles from home, not yet accustomed to the wonderful freedom of Aussie life and acceptance.

Another wonderful highlight was watching Aussie Rules football – a mixture of rugby, Gaelic football and handball, played at a furious pace in four quarters. A great game! The passion on the field was matched by the passion of the spectators. One Saturday afternoon, our third engineer, John Brown from Forest Gate, London, decided to cheer on the opposing team, whilst standing with the home crowd. It wasn't to last, as a little old lady began to beat him with her umbrella. How we laughed! John was a real comic and took it all in fun. Aussies like a drink, and after matches numerous kids, pushing old prams, would be seen collecting up empty beer bottles to sell on for a penny a time.

There was an outstanding player for Essendon, John Coleman by name, who was usually in the papers the day after a match, as his play was acrobatic, scoring many points and leaping higher than any other player. Years later, in 2003, when Helen and I were at the Ellel Ministries Centre (Gilbulla) in Sydney, I struck up a friendship with the caretaker there, who was badly crippled and asked me to pray with him. It turned out that he had been friends with John Coleman, who, sadly, had become an alcoholic and died penniless.

My experience watching Aussie Rules in Melbourne had now been used by God to forge a temporary but meaningful relationship in Gilbulla, forty-nine years later. Similar 'coincidences' seem to have happened so often. Amazing!

It was time to sail on. Boilers were fired up, engines tested. The ship was beginning to look and feel like a sea-going vessel again. Sad farewells, lots of hugs, tears, and the dreadful, sometimes wrenching break up of friendships. Would I ever return? We sailed down the Yarra for Geelong. After about a week, heavy wooden shifting boards and feeders were fitted and the *Sheilbank* was down on her marks, laden with bulk grain for India. What lay ahead was heat, poverty and the stench of Calcutta – another but different kind of culture shock.

Chapter 3
India – A Very Different Culture

We arrived at the estuary of the Hooghly River. No land to be seen, just a buoy with a pilot boat and, of course, the pilot who would take the ship the 128 miles up to the sprawling city of Calcutta (now Kolkata). What made our approach memorable for this first-timer was the number of insects of all shapes and sizes in the Bay of Bengal, even though no land was yet visible. The Sunderbans gradually appeared on the horizon – low-lying mudflats and mango groves. On we steamed, as riverbanks emerged and local river craft, some with sails, many with oars, passed both up and downstream, and to starboard a light/signal station, Suager Island.

In the days of British rule, tigers were known to swim across to the small island, hence a 303 rifle was a must. It seemed an age before the river began to narrow and the miles-wide estuary was left behind. The smell was now all-pervading, coming from the land as well as the river, and made worse by the searing heat.

I can't remember how long it took us to travel the 128 miles from the East Channel Light Vessel near Sandheads to the dock, but it must have been twelve hours or more, depending on tides and whether it was the rainy season. The monsoon rains would cause the Ganges and its many tributaries to be in full spate. What I do remember was the time it took to get the *Sheilbank* into the locks and then into Kidderpore Dock. As far as I know, all ships used compressed air to initiate engine movements, and anyone with some knowledge of such matters will be able to imagine how many times the *Sheilbank*'s triple expansion engine was required to 'go forward, stop; a touch more, stop; half astern, stop; hard-a-starboard, full ahead, stop; full astern, stop.' A coal-fired engine room gets very hot, the stokers are on the verge of collapse and finally we're alongside. Heat, heat, overwhelming heat, the engines, boilers, and of course the steam winches and capstans all adding to the heat. Even the wood in my cabin was too hot to touch.

It was 1954, and wartime-built ships like ours had no fans and no air-conditioning, just heat, steam, noise from twelve steam winches, and the cries and shouts of hundreds of coolies as they proceeded to unload the vessel. The grain was in bulk, and the method of discharge was not with mechanical grabs, but by hundreds of men filling jute sacks and using cranes and our derricks to sling them over the side on to the dock or the waterside and into barges.

Whilst here, apprentices were put on twelve hour watches – twelve on and twelve off. I was on from 0600 to 1800. Not too bad, but sleep? Even at night when it did cool a little, the porthole had to be shut to keep out wandering hands. I just lay on my bunk in pools of sweat, wondering why on earth I'd decided to go to sea. Getting out on deck for 0600 was wonderful – it was relatively cooler, until, bang on time, the huge orange ball of fire rose above the superstructure of the ship and dockside until, within minutes, the heat throbbed into every part of a steam ship with a steel hull, deck and accommodation, which very quickly became too hot to touch. Surprisingly the discharge was fast, mainly because of the hundreds of Indians working twenty-four hours. The ship rose so much higher every day as thousands of sacks of wheat seemed to be spirited away. Each sack, as it arrived on the dock, was lifted on to the head of a coolie who almost ran into the shade. Amazing strength, considering how thin and under-nourished they all looked.

But now it was time to venture ashore. A Reverend and Mrs Corlett were the shore links for Calcutta, so I phoned them and headed for Carey Baptist Church. Culture shock hit me like a ton of bricks as I tried to make my way along the dock to the dock entrance. Immediately outside sat the beggars – lame, deformed, many deliberately so in order to attract more buckshees. Exhaustion from overwork and lack of sleep, plus the stench of endlessly chewed betel nut juice, sweat and dribble, added to the assault on my senses, which by this time were screaming. I remember crying out to God for help and somehow a row of taxis beckoned. All the drivers were Sikhs – the Indian warrior race. Fierce eyes glared at me as I stuttered, "Carey Baptist Church, Bowbazar Street, please."

The church was big with tall pillars, an imposing entrance, very high ceilings and numerous fans. Walter and Mrs Corlett made me so welcome and over a period of weeks I came to know them and the church quite well. The worship there became very precious to me, not least because of the congregation – Indians from east, west, north and south. At that time Calcutta had more students in its university than anywhere else: Chinese, Anglo Indian, Burmese, American and British. The Reverend Corlett was an accomplished pianist and it was here that I first heard that wonderful song, *How Great Thou Art*. Yes, Lord, You had brought me so far to join with a hundred or more young people and others in singing it, some of whom attended Calcutta Bible College, including Archie Shear and Rupert Bunting, whose widow I was to meet in Bexhill, East Sussex sixty years later! Rupert was a jazz player with an amazing testimony of freedom from drug addiction, who became a great preacher and later moved to the UK. Also David Das, a former Hindu expelled from his family for following Jesus, and many like him. Then there was the young man who could recite the whole of St John's Gospel by heart, learning it on his way to work every day. For me, coming from a very conservative background and church, meeting and having fellowship with these amazing people was absolutely revolutionary. But what was to enrich these events even more was meeting up with the principals of Calcutta Bible College, Doctor and Mrs Cook from Oregon, USA. They really looked after me – delicious curries, and even one or two overnight stays – initially a bit scary due to lizards on the ceiling.

Meanwhile, the discharge of the *Sheilbank* cargo had been completed and we'd been moved to a river berth – again a long and very wearisome business. The anchors had to be hung off the bow either side, the anchor chain 'broken' and so many shackles let down on to flat barges. These were then ferried aft to be hauled up on deck and made fast to the bollards – a difficult, hot and exhausting job; the forward cables had to be secured to a buoy – similarly the aft chains. The ship was now secured fore and aft with her anchor chains, a clear indication of the power of the currents and tides of the Hooghly, as well as the bore tides (more of this later). Large floating warehouses came alongside with huge bales of hessian cloth made from the jute which was common in East Bengal. These were known as 'gunnies', in short, sacking for sacks. Plastic was still unknown for use as sacks.

At last, after five or six weeks, it was time to move on. On the day the ship was due to sail, Doctor and Mrs Cook's chef came to the ship with a huge American angel cake for my seventeenth birthday. I was very popular for a while! We were ready for off and set about retrieving so many shackles of anchor cable, connecting the anchors and beginning the long journey back to the estuary. There the pilot disembarked, and the *Sheilbank* was on her way to Colombo, en route for Durban, South Africa. What cargo space had been left was quickly filled with cases of tea and desiccated coconut and, some weeks later, The Bluff, which marked the port entrance to Durban Harbour, gradually loomed on the horizon.

In 1954 The Bluff was bare of any buildings – just a grassy, raised natural barrier protecting the city which lay behind it. On the south side of the harbour entrance was a whaling factory. Whales were still hunted by small, fast boats with the harpoon gun mounted in the bows. Often the whales were tied alongside the narrow seawall entrance and the smell was pretty strong. The city was great, but apartheid was still practised: 'white only' buses, toilets and cinemas. It seemed to be the norm and, generally speaking, I saw no violence. However, I became personally involved in the system when a black African docker was arrested for theft. With my authorisation he had collected a small quantity of tea 'sweepings' (more dust than tea) to take home. The ship had completed discharge. Could he have some of the sweepings? "Yes," I had said, also checking with the shoreside hatch manager. However, the guard on the dock gate decided he had stolen it. I was asked to go to court, thinking I could defend him. When the opportunity came I was told to sit down and shut up. He was fined and imprisoned for three months.

The 'blacks', as they were then known, a derogatory and totally unacceptable term at that time, were in small townships, and I can remember tales of drunkenness, the result of a powerful brew mixed up in 40-gallon drums and spiced up with old car batteries! Natal was very cosmopolitan in that era – British, Dutch settlers, Africans, of course – many tribes, but mostly Zulus in the Durban area, who were the dockworkers. Then the Indians, thousands of whom had been transported from India to work the sugar cane plantations. I think it fair to say that the diversity and cultures of all these different groups of peoples together brought colour, but also tensions, to the area.

In Durban, yet again through shore links, I met a Christian family who welcomed me. The son, Ronnie Gibson, of Scottish origin, was a few years older than me. His interest lay in guitar playing, and so my conservative 'English Christianity' eyes were opened yet again when, after church one Sunday, off came Ronnie's suit, and bare-footed, he met up with African buskers, to jam with them, learning African rhythms. He was a chemist and had worked for three months on a whaling factory ship, which had spent some time nearer to Antarctica than the Cape. I have many fond memories of Durban where I went to the cinema to see Alfred Hitchcock's film *Psycho;* shared in an open-air gospel meeting in the town hall square; enjoyed my first open-air cinema (a 'drive-in'); and, as usual, met another young lady – this time one of Ronnie's cousins who lived in Pinetown.

So much for Durban. Once discharged, we changed berth to the coal wharf where we took on a full cargo of coal for no less a place than Aden, right at the southern end of the Red Sea. Our ship was a coal-burner so coal bunkers were on hand. Once the loaded hatches were battened down and decks washed down (though mostly done at sea), we made our way north to the farthest north-eastern tip of Africa. With the island of Socotra on our starboard beam we steamed into the Gulf of Aden and tied up to buoys in the harbour which was to be our home for six weeks.

Aden was a major bunkering port for shipping. Most ships, having steamed through the Suez Canal en route for India, the Far East and Australia, used Aden to take on fresh water and bunkers, although the former always tasted stale.

In 1954 the town was small, just a row of shops and houses. In fact, the *only* green to be seen were strips of grass and a few trees outside the shops. The surrounding land was bare, barren volcanic rock – just nothing to feast your eyes on. Nearer the port entrance was the NAAFI club for British military, but we were not allowed in – military only, the Merchant Navy being considered riff raff. So, what to do? Zilch! Along with another apprentice and a couple of others, I attempted a bit of 'mountaineering', but the wild dogs roaming around there were a source of real concern, as to be bitten would almost certainly have resulted in rabies.

So, this was our fate: three weeks of discharging coal then, believe it or not, a thorough wash down, particularly the holds, which were then whitewashed before three more weeks of loading sea salt, of all things. Imagine the heat – the very reason for the salt, as large areas of shallow sea water were trapped and then allowed to evaporate, resulting in the valuable salt for export. As usual, our discomfort was increased by the additional heat from the boilers and steam winches. We looked on with envy as other ships – some passenger and others fast cargo carriers to Australia and New Zealand – came and went within hours. A cooling swim would have been nice, but I have no memory of swimming in the sea. I guess it was dangerous.

Finally, the day came when the Plimsoll line indicated that we were fully laden. Hatches were battened down, buoys released fore and aft, and with smoke belching from the funnel we were on our way again, relishing the breeze outside the harbour and en route for Japan via Ceylon (now Sri Lanka) and Colombo, where we bunkered again before navigating the Malacca and Singapore Straits and continuing north-east towards Kobe, Japan. Some years later I was the officer responsible for navigation and, as any map will show, there are scores of islands and nations in the Far East, making the task very demanding, but also exciting. Then throw in a major typhoon to add to the excitement of being a seafarer in a tatty tramp ship!

Chapter 4
Tramping the World

Every Saturday the master inspected all areas of the ship, including the apprentices' accommodation. This usually resulted in failure, as our carefully packed drawers were turned upside down on the floor and Saturday p.m. leave (a rarity intended as study leave) cancelled, subject to it being done all over again. And then something special: an hour on the bridge, learning how to steer by compass – one magnetic compass on the monkey island and one in the wheelhouse. In those days we had no radar, no gyro, but a primitive echo sounder. On leaving port we always 'streamed the log' and then took readings daily, always at noon, to coincide with noon 'sights'. Incidentally, the log was not a tree trunk but a brass finned rotor streamed from aft, which revolved and, being attached to a meter, recorded the distance covered. Ten knots was the norm and the journey just went on and on. I often wondered if land would ever appear again. It did, but we were now steaming towards Colombo, Ceylon, across the Arabian Sea (in the northern Indian Ocean).

Bunkering in Colombo didn't take long and I think it was on this visit that I made contact with a Mr D'Alwes. He was yet another member of Living Links and a senior port official. I had had no Christian fellowship since Durban. Again there was just a short visit to Singapore before we were off again on our relentless tramping, north into the North Pacific Ocean and eventually Japan. A few years later I was to regularly visit Japan, so more of its delights and shocks to come.

By this time home was a distant memory. I no longer felt homesick or let the odd tear escape as I lay in my bunk, especially as word got out that we would soon be completing our discharge in Japan and making our way south to load guano phosphate (bird poo!) and then on to Australia. Nauru (Pleasant Island) is a small island almost on the equator, and was in the process of being dug out. Centuries of bird droppings were now eagerly wanted as fertiliser for the thousands of square acres of Australian farmland.

(Nowadays the Islanders are really struggling with health and with what is left of the island, since its heart has been dug out.)

Nauru was also home to South Sea Islanders who had amazing physiques, with equally big personalities, always smiling and laughing, and who would row out to the ship every morning garlanded with flowers, the position and type of the garlands indicating their status – engaged, married or 'available'!

The ship tied up to two buoys, fore and aft, as a huge cantilever swung over, loading 10,000 tons of guano in just a few days.

Soon *Sheilbank*, fully loaded down to her marks (Plimsoll) and probably a bit over, slipped her buoys and steamed almost due south for 1000 miles to the port of Newcastle, NSW Australia. Ships were required to be 'on their marks' on arrival in port, but some masters allowed for the use of water, fuel and pumping out water tanks en route for trim. You can imagine the scene: we were covered in grey dust from stem to stern, but hosing down was popular, especially in the tropics. We didn't know at the time, but *Sheilbank*, an ideal bulk carrier, was to spend six to eight months on the phosphate trade route, sometimes loading at Ocean Island in the Central Pacific Ocean, and known today as Kiribati.

For probably all of us on board, although the work was hard and dirty, it was a great run, as the weather was wonderful and, as for me, I was able to get to know a Christian family in Newcastle, which in 1954 was a small port town in typical Victorian style with one main street. So many memories.

An elderly shore link, Mr Mcleod, introduced me to a much younger family nearby, with a son and daughter, telling me that Australian education was so much better than British! But oh, what a joy it was to jump into a taxi at the dockside, knowing a warm Christian welcome awaited me. The taxi cost one shilling a flagfall and a shilling a mile in the notorious Aussie Holden, which was known as the 'crumple car' as it had a reputation for 'crumpling' in any collision.

I couldn't wait for Sunday, hoping for a day off to have the opportunity to attend church. It duly came, but I was in for a shock: dear

Mr McCleod explained to me that I would not be allowed to participate in communion because I didn't have a 'letter of commendation'. I also had to sit at the back. (I probably feel more indignation about this now than then.) Their hospitality was second to none. I came to love Newcastle. The Seamen's Mission was great; lovely girls encouraged us on to the dance floor, then, sometime during the evening, a ship's bell rang and we were gripped and led firmly into the chapel! Many Missions worldwide had godly chaplains, but the one in Newcastle was quite sad, gabbling through a couple of prayers and then rushing to the door to be first to escape. Most of us found it quite amusing. After some time at sea, sitting next to a nubile young lady made it all worthwhile.

Unloading and discharging phosphate was a messy business, as cranes and the ship's derricks loaded it onto railway trucks and lorries – no neat containers in those days. This was my first encounter with a 'fair dinkum Aussie wharfie'. Billy cans were brewed on deck over a small primus stove, but to me, a first year apprentice officer whose *monthly* wage was £5.12s 6d, their *hourly* wage, after midnight, of 19s 11d, won by a recent strike, was mind-blowing.

I can't remember how many times we went to Nauru during this, my first voyage. Sometimes we returned to Port Kembla just south of Sydney and on to Melbourne. Eventually Bank Line owners decided that the *Sheilbank* should load grain from Port Kembla or nearby Geelong and then return to Calcutta, which in reality was our home port. The ship was therefore cleaned, particularly the holds, and the erection of shifting boards, again by a gang of twenty to thirty carpenters, prepared the ship for her cargo, which was poured into the ship via huge chutes and didn't take long. I should explain here that, unlike today's container transports, a ship's safety in my day depended on the officer responsible knowing exactly how each type of cargo should be loaded and transported. For example, grain, if not carefully loaded in compartments created by the aforementioned shifting boards, would simply shift according to the movement of the ship, leading to dangerous destabilisation. Once ready, moorings were released fore and aft, the pilot saw us safely out of the port, and the good old tramp ship, once again belching black smoke over our freshly hosed decks, began the long voyage to India through the Bass

Strait, calm this time, across the Australian Bight, again notorious for bad weather, and off on a north-westerly heading for the Bay of Bengal. Once again, we crossed the equator.

As apprentices we were constantly chipping and painting, cleaning paintwork and learning to strip down blocks and grease running gear, then taking turns at steering. In bad weather we cleaned and painted the inside accommodation, stripped wood, sanded and varnished it and checked the lifeboats with the third mate. All lifeboat gear had to be checked, but although the dried biscuits were in tins, one look led us to hope we would never have to eat them! Swinging from the mast in a bosun's chair whilst the ship pitched and rolled and we were trying to paint was not a favourite task either. Then there was the taking of turns on watch as lookout, learning navigation, holy stoning the wooden deck (yet again), brass polishing etc.

Over the long weeks, tired weak muscles became stronger, although I can remember being a bit worried as I was still as skinny as a rake and hardly sweated, so I repeatedly took on heavier work if available but alas, I think my genes kept me thin. When working on deck in the heat, it was normal for us to wear only shorts and flipflops and now, in my seventies and eighties, I am reaping the consequences of skin damage brought about by those tropical days at sea.

I haven't said much about the weather. As mentioned, *Sheilbank* was bottom heavy – a very 'stiff' ship, rolling and pitching, sliding and slipping down the waves. The huge waves of the Southern Ocean gave way to the calms of the Tropics. It became very hot – no fans or air-conditioning (what was that?!) but we chugged on doggedly, making our way day after day at about 10 knots, and now and again picking up a current, and then, on the port bow saw Ceylon – a good landmark. By this time the rain and unpleasantness of the south-westerly monsoon told us we were steaming once again into the Bay of Bengal, where the pilot vessel met us at the mouth of the Hooghly River and then hours and hours of standby, hours and hours of weariness, the heat and wet of the monsoon adding to the heat of the engines until we were alongside, and what seemed to be a thousand coolies swarmed aboard. Hatches opened, gunnie sacks in the thousands were filled with grain and swung ashore by crane and onto floating warehouses alongside. And, of course, twenty-four hour working; the roar and heat of winches; the shouting and noise of the workforce. Then suddenly, because of the rain, the cry would go up, "A beam le gow!" (or that's what it sounded like), hatch beams would be swung into place, large tarpaulins lifted over the hatch and work stopped, waiting for the rain to stop. But, here in Calcutta was Calcutta Bible College and the inspiring students, love and fellowship, being spoilt and the occasional night ashore in the college.

Because of the number of coolies the discharge didn't take too long, and then we shifted berth to the river, where it was cooler, but often nights and days of sleep were lost due to huge bore tides. To see a 7000 ton cargo ship lifted right out of the water, anchor chains snapped and the ship swept up river towards Howrah Bridge by a 40 foot wave, was amazing and a bit scary too. We had to be on standby quite some time before the wave was due. Then it would come racing round the bend in the river, breaking over the banks and sweeping everything before it. Why Indians stood on the bank I'll never know – maybe for a religious reason – but many died. Amazingly, the small Indian crafts rode the bore, seemingly with ease. Without a doubt the Indian seamen were very good. And so it all died down again, anchor cables were slackened off, loading continued and yet again we were loading gunnies from large floating warehouses on either side of the ship. This took a while, as it was vital that no bale touched the iron/steel surface of the ship since condensation would ruin the cloth. Timber and hessian matting did a good job to protect it, but it was a constant job to ensure it was used.

Our next destination was to be South Africa, but not before Colombo, where we loaded tea, desiccated coconut, coconut oil and of course more coal bunkers, and then headed for Cape Town where, unusually, eleven passengers were to embark for Tristan da Cunha – a small island in the South Atlantic. Our cargo was for Buenos Aires, Argentina, plus a few hundred tons for Montevideo, Uruguay. We hoped to be in Buenos Aires for Christmas – now Christmas 1954.

By now a whole year had gone by.

Sea conditions vary a lot, of course, from the fairly steady but wet and warm weather of the south-westerly monsoon to the calms of the equatorial latitudes and the fresh, bracing winds of the South Indian Ocean. Having weathered Madagascar without any landfall, we battled on slowly towards the South African coast, eventually picking up the strong Agulhas current. We always knew we were there, as the swells increased in size, the remnant of southerly storms straight from the Southern Ocean and Antarctic. The current, moving south from the equator, met the blasts from the Antarctic and produced dangerous seas. *Sheilbank* was simply hell to be on in these conditions. Once again we learnt to cope with walking on the bottom of the bulkheads (i.e. on the walls) before being slammed back again. Years later I was to meet a South African Airforce pilot whose job was to fly over a large area of the South African coast reporting weather and sea conditions. Many ships, even larger ones, had foundered in what at times were freak conditions in this area.

We finally rounded Cape Agulhas and the Cape of Good Hope and thankfully steamed into Cape Town docks. Stores for Tristan da Cunha and the aforementioned passengers were quickly loaded, but we were not usually a passenger ship, so who were these passengers? They turned out to be Tristan's new administrator and his wife, the island doctor with his wife and three children, and four islanders, one of whom had been in hospital in Cape Town. We had a hospital and a number of passenger cabins on the *Sheilbank*, as the ship had been built for the war. I think another of the passengers was the manager of a South African crayfish company based on Tristan who was returning from leave. The islanders, who spoke 'pigeon', were strong and muscular. We then moved on to the bunkering wharf before, only too quickly, we were once again at sea, on a course west-south-west for Tristan. Table Mountain, with all its mystery and grandeur, gradually slipped below the horizon, as *Sheilbank* made slow progress heading into the 'roaring forties', a constant force 4 to 6 and sometimes stronger winds dead against our course, as the sea drift followed the wind. I guess our 10 knots was reduced to about 8.

Then one day a dark smudge appeared on the starboard bow: Tristan da Cunha. We had somehow made it. Today, a navigating officer simply walks into the chart room and reads off the exact position of the ship in latitude and longitude, but for us the sextant and daily 'sights' were the tools of the trade, along with the echo sounder. Often, in bad weather, the absence of sun or stars brought out the best of experience and seamanship from the 'Old Man' and the second mate, the ancient art of 'dead reckoning' proving their skills again and again.

Tristan is a volcanic island 1500 miles south-south-west from Cape Town, easily recognised by its distinctive cone shape. In the early 1960s the volcano erupted and all the islanders were evacuated, many to the UK. Since then, many have returned and the population now numbers around three hundred. It's said to be the most remote island in the world, and if you Google Tristan today you will see a small harbour, motor vehicles and small power craft. I'm not sure if we tied up to a solitary buoy or simply dropped anchor – the seabed must have been suitable enough to hold the flukes of the anchor. The islanders rowed large long-boats made of canvas with wooden ribs and keel sourced from another island, as no trees grew on Tristan. Discharging supplies and passengers was a great feat of seamanship, particularly as long rollers caused the boats alongside to plunge into the troughs and then ride to the crest. The right time to lower precious goods and people was critical if we didn't want to dump them in the water, but all was achieved.

We were told that the surrounding sea was rich in fish, so a couple of apprentices had a go. "Line or hook?"

"Better this way," an islander said. "Catch a fish and beat it on the ship's side, letting the pulverised fish fall into the sea."

Within minutes what seemed to be thousands of fish surrounded the ship. All the men had to do was lower a bucket over the side and pull it up, full of fish. The chief steward was very happy to renew old fish stocks with the fresh variety! In addition, as a goodwill gesture from the crayfish factory, our freezer was filled with large crayfish, although I don't think we lower, junior mortals ever tasted one. During our stay here (1954) a number of us bought a set of Tristan stamps which I still have somewhere.

Cargoes and passengers ashore, No. 3 hatch battened down, anchor hove to and *Sheilbank* was off again, her voyage set almost due west towards the Argentine coast. The weather improved as the sun broke out, bringing the warmth of a Mediterranean climate, roughly in the 30 degrees north latitude, and repeated in the Southern Atlantic Ocean 30 degrees south latitude. Cleaning the salt off the ship and painting kept us busy, as always, but most of all was a growing excitement and anticipation of arriving in South America. Eventually, those with radios picked up that most exciting of Latin beats – the Argentinian tango. A few days east of destination saw a change in the sea, particularly at night: the churn of the propellor became alight with sparkling phosphorous as the water broke at the bow, then alongside, and then aft.

The landfall was low-lying, speed reduced, crew and engine on standby and pristine uniforms donned, replacing casual deck and work wear. The mid-channel marker buoy appeared and, of course, the pilot boat. A number of pilots came aboard to be returned to port, having left ships outward bound. Here the backhanders of tea from Ceylon paved the way as they changed hands with skippers of the pilot boat and whoever else was deemed to be 'important'. President Peron was still alive and well in the Argentine, and he forbade the import of foreign tea. Although we carried a few hundred tons, the local folk were obliged to drink their own homegrown 'green' tea. More later, but first we were to call in at Montevideo and there in the river, not far from shore, were the masts of the *Graf Spee*.

For those who don't know, the *Graf Spee* was a German battle cruiser in the well-documented Battle of the River Plate. Outside the estuary, British ships were waiting for her should she put to sea. In 1939 she was scuttled with her fuel system badly damaged and sixteen years later the tops of her masts could still be seen.

Another shore link lived in Montevideo – a Mr Boyd. We had little time there and did not make contact except by phone. Our third engineer, a Londoner like me, with a great sense of humour, persuaded me to accompany him to the Roman Catholic cathedral. This was a huge building and packed out, but we managed to squeeze in at the back. What with Latin and Spanish we hadn't a clue what it was all about, except that it definitely wasn't Baptist! Our stay was short and our journey to Buenos Aires began.

The pilotage turned out to be very eventful. I have a strong recollection of the pilot boasting of how good he was, bringing on juniors to take over when required. The time came for 'hands' to, "Stand by – first mate for'ard, second mate aft, third mate bridge." In theory the 'Old Man' was in charge and had the authority to overrule the pilot. However, he didn't know the port and river conditions, so obviously the pilot was responsible for the ship's safe passage. My place was on the bridge – available to run any messages. *Sheilbank* did have a few phones, but still relied on the blowtube and whistle to communicate – amazing when you compare this with modern smartphones. In the Argentine, a number of attempted coups had taken place, but President Peron was still in power and it was he who was responsible for the building of the new dock we were steaming into. However, it didn't take too much pilotage ability to see that our ship was steaming too fast towards our berth. I could see the first mate making frantic signals from the fo'c'sle head and hear him screaming, "Shall I drop the anchor?" but still no pilot response. Seeing what was about to happen, the 'Old Man' took over, ordering, "Reverse engine," but the weight of a fully loaded 10,000 ton ship takes a lot of stopping. With no room to manoeuvre in the dock, we smashed right into the stern of an Argentinian passenger ship about to leave port and, instead of avoiding a disaster, the order to "Drop anchor" resulted in the anchor being dropped right on to the rudder of the passenger ship as we came to a shuddering halt, with our bows stoved in and badly damaged, plus considerable damage to the stern of the other ship. I can remember holding my sides to stop myself laughing outright, and, as for the pilot, his boasts proved somewhat exaggerated.

(A recent TV documentary investigating the cause of the Suez Canal disaster when this vital shipping link was blocked by a super-sized container ship, the *Ever Given*, showed just what can happen if the master and pilot do not work well together, and reminded me vividly of the above event.)

Buenos Aires was one of the most exciting places I was ever to visit. The city, as far as night life was concerned, never woke up before 2300hrs. Cargo was worked during daylight hours, except for 1200 to 1400, when siesta gave us a break from the heat of a southern hemisphere summer's day. We three apprentices just couldn't wait to get ashore. It was cooler at night, of course, and we developed a system allowing us to experience the magic of Buenos Aires to the full. Everywhere we went we were invaded by the beat of the Argentinian tango as it throbbed, charging the atmosphere with excitement and promise, added to which, Christmas wasn't far off.

It was 1954. Eva Peron had died in 1952 and nearly all the streets in Buenos Aires were named after either Juan Peron or Eva Peron. The British had been responsible for the building of the railway system and the main Retiro Station which was now renamed President Peron Station. It was quite common to hear gunfire somewhere in the city, although I never saw any of the rebels. On a later trip to Buenos Aires the port was under curfew, and armed guards with loaded pistols stood by the gangway after 2100hrs. They also carried boleros – two hard spheres attached to a length of line, which were mainly used by gauchos and thrown to bring down cattle. We were told they were never very accurate, but were used if you tried to run away.

If you've seen the play or film of *Evita* you will have some idea of the sense of excitement, fear and adventure that pervaded the city known as the Paris of South America. How to be part of this mad mad world where the official exchange rate was 40 pesos to the pound? But we could send home for sterling which had a street price of 70 pesos to the pound, and British shipping companies had regular routes to the UK, in particular the Royal Mail Cargo and Blue Star companies.

Our days there went something like this:

- 0700 on deck to work
- 1200-1300 lunch and sleep
- 1700 knock off, shower and crash in bunk
- 2300 off ashore to taste the crazy city life
- 0500 next day a 7UP and a large beef steak at the dock gate café (3 pesos) and hit the sack until turnout on deck for 0700

The shore link in Buenos Aires was a Mr and Mrs Lear, with a married daughter who worked in the city, and whose husband owned a company making shoe polish. The two sons, John and Bruce, were a little older than me and both owned Vincent 1000cc motorbikes; they were also members of the Tigris Rowing Club and the family lived in Belgrano, a Buenos Aires suburb, home to many English and Germans. Memories include sitting through a Sunday service, all in Spanish, with Mr Lear stopping from time to time to explain to me in English what he was preaching, and then later helping Mrs Lear to prepare the largest fruit salad I'd ever seen in my life.

It was Christmas in the southern hemisphere and very hot. The journey from the docks to Belgrano was scary and interesting. Bruce arrived to collect me on his Vincent, and off we went at top speed, with me hanging on for dear life. The traffic was crazy, and the method for turning left or right was to get the bike far enough ahead of buses, cars or lorries, then simply turn. The alternative transport also had its problems, due to language restraints. Small buses known as 'collectives', like small minibuses, were jammed solid with passengers. It was one thing to get on, but having then found yourself pushed towards the rear, it was quite another to get off. So, you had to know your destination and start early, elbowing your way to the front whilst yelling in your best Spanish, "Permisso, permisso!" and with luck you'd be catapulted out on to the pavement – in my case, outside President Peron Station. And remember, all this was against the background of civil unrest – very exciting for a young teenager from a rather staid London suburb. Bruce taught me where to go in the station and how to ask for a ticket – so here goes: "Belgrano, ida-e-velta premera, senor," (or something like that!) and it usually went okay. (Translation: "First class return ticket to Belgrano.") The trains reminded me of the ones seen in Westerns in as much as the entrance to the carriage was very wide, and it was quite normal for passengers to board or alight along the line if the train was slow enough. On one occasion the train was pulling out of the station with me, as usual, standing near the open end, but this time I was caught out when a man came racing down the platform and, arriving abreast of me, started yelling out something to me in Spanish. All I could do was yell back, "No comprendo," but, regardless, he jumped on, only to find out he had boarded the wrong train! It took him quite a while to calm down, but soon I was off and looking forward to more fellowship, food and fun with the family.

When not visiting the Lear family I went ashore with the other apprentices. We enjoyed the seamen's clubs, in particular Christmas dinners in the Roman Catholic and Church of England Missions. The girls were heavily chaperoned, but I was always struck by the way they dressed – generally in pretty summer dresses, in stark contrast to the dull clothes and headscarves of the post war British girls back home. And then again there was the throb and mystery of the tango, the warmth and a romantic moon, all of which made it easy to be in a wonderland and so very remote from the cold and wet of the UK.

Our way back to the ship was always via a funfair. I'm sure folks there thought we were crazy, but I've often thought about one particular ride: it had a vertical arm with a motor in the centre and a cockpit at either end. Once in, the only means of security was a chain fastened around the waist and off we went, first horizontally then vertically, literally hanging upside down on the chain. I really do believe Father looked after me as, by today's standards, it was truly a death-trap. Once off the ride it was a snack at the dock gates and then back to the cabin to crash out until the 0700 turn-to.

Avenida 9 de Julio is (or was?) the widest avenue in the world and crossing it was quite an achievement. On one occasion I was instructed to escort a number of the crew to the doctor's. Lascars preferred to walk in single file, and you can imagine my embarrassment as I led a long line of them, like a mother duck with her ducklings; it felt as if half of Buenos Aires was staring at us! I was also asked to accompany the men into the consultations. Did I speak Hindi? No, only a few words. One of the crew did not return to the ship, as he had a large growth protruding from his chest which had been there for some time. In no way should he have been allowed to sail from Calcutta three months earlier when we changed crews, but bribery was common in the depths of the shipping clerks' offices there.

On a rare day off the weather was perfect, with wonderful clear skies, and Bruce came down to the ship to take me out. I had expressed a desire to buy a classical guitar. The town was hot and busy, prompting a visit to a coffee shop (not at all common in the UK in 1954). Bruce ordered. Needless to say I was very hot and weary, but not for long; South American caffeine took over and I was soon as high as a kite, trying to contain my new-found energy on the crowded streets. For £8 we bought a lovely guitar which I still have today, although it's now cracked, since being taken into a London school by my brand new wife in 1970.

One other outstanding experience was a train journey of a couple of hours, out into the beginnings of the Pampas region. The Lears had friends in a small community there and it was fun being met with a horse and buggy. It was very very dusty, and gauchos could be seen riding their ponies with the boleros attached to their waists. I also went to the cinema in Corrientes – a famous road in Buenos Aires, where I saw *The Robe*, a popular Christian film, widely shown in secular cinemas back home as well.

Well, back to seafaring. The cargo of gunnies was discharged and shifting boards were again installed in the holds before loading 10,000 tons of maize for Europe, all of which took a few days. Some of the Chinese crew members, having previously prepared cages, saw this as an opportunity to climb nearby cranes and capture a number of pigeons, in order to enjoy their eggs. I always used to say that if I were ever shipwrecked, I would prefer to be with Chinese companions, as they seem to know how to survive anywhere.

The damage to the ship's bows had by now been patched up for our return to the northern hemisphere, but the crew were worried about her: "Oh, Saab, very dangerous; ship no good go through Bay of Biscay!" Finally, all holds battened down, a good head of steam in the boilers, John Brown (yes, really) smoking one of his many pipes and gleefully switching off the fans in the boiler space when the steam pressure dropped, and we were off.

After a few weeks, the wonderful weather gave way to the equatorial doldrums, and then the cold Atlantic depressions signalled our return to the Western Approaches. We saw the Land's End light and probably the Sovereign Light Vessel, but the port of Antwerp we were headed for was in Belgium where, after discharge, the ship would go into dry dock for repairs, painting and a mass of other needs to be attended to. But the sea hadn't finished with us yet.

We paid off, went by train to the Hook of Holland and embarked on a small British Rail cross-Channel ferry. Punching into a full-blooded North Sea gale was wretched. We had accommodation in the bows for the night crossing, and the pitching was so severe that we were lifted clear out of our bunks and then dropped back down with a thud. The second mate – a hardened Aussie – declared it was the worst sea experience of his life. As for me, I was terribly seasick and so returned home in the freezing cold, feeling exhausted, tired and hungry. But I was home. It felt very strange. My payslips indicated that I had signed on 23.09.53 and paid off 08.02.55, aged almost eighteen – a first trip which had lasted 16 months and 17 days. My total basic earnings were £118.19s 5d, with total deductions £79 5s

10d and extra allowances paid for Sundays at sea (double pay). In all I was the proud owner of £57.0s.2d and in theory was due 62 and a half days' leave. Still, I suppose a bus fare was only 2d (tuppence).

So, I was now back home, but trying to fit in at home was not easy. Many of the friends I had previously known at church had moved away (even more so after my next trip) and a lot of the lads were away on National Service – in those days an obligatory two year Armed Forces training period for young men. As I looked back, I could see that God had kept me every step of the way but I had met Christians in a number of countries and had realised that many of the taboos in a UK Baptist church were not the same as elsewhere, so that was another factor making it difficult to fit in. Still, it was good to be back: home-cooking, a tiny bedroom of my own, but little personal space in 3 Sylvester Road, London N2. I had changed and obviously grown up a bit, but Mum and Dad didn't like my late hours or the overuse of electricity, and the reality was that I was desperately lonely, and so continued the ever-growing sense of 'not belonging'. The church young people were great, but all had their own relationships by now. Who could I talk to? Relate to? Share with? From memory, I think there was one person who was kind and caring but… I was almost eighteen and began developing a protective facade: *I'm fine... no problem... Look what a wonderful person I am... been round the world* etc. Few had experienced such travel in 1955. There was no real conversation at home and Mum and Dad weren't folks to share thoughts and feelings. It was to be many years before I discovered who I really was. I had not the slightest idea that my Heavenly Dad had given me a distinct identity. Heck – what on earth was identity anyway? So I learnt to rely on my 'celebrity' status. Dear Mum and Dad, I loved them so much. If only they'd found communication easier.

Chapter 5

Two onions? Put one back!/ A Very Unhappy Ship

All too soon the dreaded brown envelope arrived:

> JOIN TITANBANK IN LIVERPOOL ON 25TH MARCH 1955. TRAVEL VOUCHERS INCLUDED.

My second trip was upon me. My leave had been one month and seventeen days. Gladstone Dock in Liverpool was busy but, as usual for Bank Line ships, the company did not trade outward from the UK. Once again we were heading for New Orleans but with a huge difference: this voyage was to last almost 26 months.

In this chapter I will simply record the main events. The ship was similar in size and origin of purpose to the *Sheilbank*. She was a USA-built liberty boat, formerly named *Samnegros*. These ships were mass-produced in the States, but the design of hull and engine was the brainchild of J L Thompsons of Sunderland; it had a triple expansion engine but was oil fuelled. They had a reputation for breaking in half, with the foredeck of three hatches parting from the accommodation and the aft two hatches, a cheerful and encouraging piece of information I received just before I was due to embark! Bulk carriers used during the war were highly suited to Bank Line cargoes. On this occasion the crew was white British. It turned out that many of these would have failed to be taken on by any decent shipping line. I was one of four apprentices and it soon became apparent that four 'slaves' were necessary for all that lay before us.

The captain turned out to be a poor choice: young, remote and posh, he found great difficulty relating to a rough crew. Food quickly became a source of discontent, and as time went on, the chief steward was found to be doing deals with providers in different ports.

Our cabins were on the bridge deck. On one side of the bridge was the chartroom; facing aft was the master's cabin with the radio officer's quarters, including his wireless room, or 'shack', as it was known. Also part of the bridge accommodation were the two-man apprentices' cabins on the portside, which were quite good.

On this ship the apprentices were under the authority of the bosun for all deck work. He was quite a character, small in stature, as tough as nails and, when drunk, he walked with a starboard list and one closed eye. Unusually, he only became seasick when not on board, but still managed to drink. The first mate (chief officer) also had alcohol problems. The second mate was much older and had spent a lot of time in India and consequently, at mealtimes, was in the habit of taking the top off the pepper pot and sprinkling pepper liberally on everything. The third mate was young and this was his first trip as an officer. The 'sparks' (radio officer) was Irish, full of fun and spent many a late watch telling tales of the Garda and the pony and cart which, even if the driver were drunk, would always find its way home – stopping at every pub on the way, of course. Engine room staff consisted of a chief plus three engineers. No coal meant no stokers, but these were replaced with 'greasers'.

You may well have gained the impression that alcohol was readily available on ships, but in fact *Titanbank* was a 'dry' ship. I sometimes wonder if this contributed to the difficulty crew members had holding their drink when ashore.

The voyage to Mississippi passed normally. The bosun worked us hard but fairly, though naturally, any really dirty jobs came our way, as apprentices were required to undertake any tasks they might subsequently, as fully-fledged officers, ask of their crew. On arrival the fun started; the ship was directed to a floating dry dock, a little downstream from New Orleans. It was very hot and the pilotage was plagued with mosquitoes which attacked us mercilessly, so the bosun, who called us his 'boys', got a Flit gun full of kerosene and squirted us all over. The pilot was very proud of his city and, on being asked why nothing had been done about the mozzies, informed us that the fishermen relied on them to attract the fish.

Once safely in the dock for routine underwater painting, the likes and dislikes of the crew began to emerge, fuelled by drink. A number of fights broke out, the worst being between the second cook and the ship's carpenter – someone to steer clear of at the best of times, as he was a nasty bit of work when sober, and very dangerous when drunk. The bad blood between the two of them resulted in the cook trying to knife the chippy, who was much bigger and always carried a large maul hammer around with him, so he soon 'downed' the cook. In fact, it would doubtless have resulted in murder if help hadn't arrived, but in the process a number of crew members sustained significant cuts and bruises. I can still see a crew member seeking out the second mate for needle and suture thread, and then proceeding to sew up the wounds as if he were just a sack. No anaesthetic, of course, local or otherwise. As apprentices we learned very quickly to stay clear, keep our mouths shut and, even more importantly, to be 'crew' and *not* apprenticed officers. We kept sawn-off broom handles to hand in our cabins, as well as always locking the door.

Ashore, the city was a bus ride away and I was keen to find a church. On leaving the ship I was amused to note that dock security was in the hands of the famous Pinkerton agents. (Those of my generation may remember the Pinkerton detectives who featured in early western films.) I remember asking the way out and was told to follow the prostrate bodies of the crew members who hadn't made it back from the first boozer outside the gates! And this was only the beginning. A tramp ship plus a white crew? Not a good place to be, let alone as part of the crew. As for the captain, he withdrew to his cabin issuing commands and threats which fell on deaf ears.

We stayed a few days in dry dock and then proceeded to a smaller port to load thousands of tons of drum oil for New Zealand. The reason for four apprentices became clearer as we were assigned to 'gangway watch'. Usually this was the role given to senior crew, but as most of the crew were drunk, it fell to us. We shared the gangway watch between us – six hour watches, the worst being the long night hours from 0000 to 0600. An already tipsy bosun (remember, we were under his authority) declared, "If you look after me I'll look after you," and off he went, already listing to starboard, with one eye closed. Our job was, of course, security, checking who might want to come on board, but also checking the mooring ropes, which had to be adjusted according to tidal highs and lows, to keep the ship safely alongside.

On one occasion, I was well into the 1800 to 0000 watch, when the captain appeared. He was going ashore and came to check the safety of the gangway ladder and safety net. We then had a very strange conversation: I was to report to him if things started to get out of hand, and not to worry because he had 'the necessary armament'! All masters carried a revolver in the captain's safe, and our captain was saying that he was prepared to use it if necessary. I guess I was responsible for sharing this piece of juicy information with the bosun on his return. It wasn't long before the 'galley wireless' picked this up and from then on the practical jokers took over. The next morning the main noticeboard bore several comic cut-outs of the Wild West and the words 'He leapt to his feet and drew his 45'. During this time, the chippy was summoned and ordered to build a solid wooden door blocking off the passage between the bridge and captain's cabin. On regular occasions, a crew member with DTs (delirium tremens) would make his way to the captain's cabin, cursing and swearing and banging on the door. Of course he was charged and fined, but that made little difference. Eventually we sailed for New Zealand via the Panama Canal, but the final straw that really sent the captain ballistic was when yet another comic magazine cut-out turned up – this time tucked inside the compass binnacle. The safety of the ship depended on respecting this vital navigational instrument.

Food was very poor. It later transpired that the chief steward was fiddling the books, a situation that eventually led to a mutiny (more later) on our arrival at Port Chalmers (Dunedin), in South Island, New Zealand.

As apprenticed officers, we were required to change for dinner and of course dine with the other officers in the saloon. We sat together on a separate table, opposite the master, chief officer, chief engineer and first mate. Arriving at dinner one day, I saw that the main course that day was stuffed onions, served as usual by the saloon steward. Unlike on Indian crew ships, where hungry apprentices could always fill up on the crew's curry, stuffed onions didn't really seem as if they would fill much of a hole, and remember, we were still in our teens and growing. Anyway, yours truly took two. That did it.

"Two onions?" the master roared across the room. "Put one back!" All eyes were directed at me and I just wished the deck would open up and swallow me. The atmosphere in the saloon reflected the unhappiness that was now characteristic of the *Titanbank*; an unhappy ship is not a good place to be on a five to six week Pacific crossing.

Gradually the crew settled down. Alcohol was forbidden whilst at sea, but discontent was rife, and the Old Man was hated for his pompous, high-handed behaviour. We were all regarded as scum, or at least, that's how it felt. Again, as apprentices, we were given most of the dirty jobs, but the bosun was true to his word and looked after us: "Just steer clear of the carpenter."

As a Christian, I found reading my Bible and remembering good times of fellowship and family were enough. Looking back, I marvel at the way my Heavenly Father kept me despite foul language and rough talk, graphic stories of brothels and conquests. Having the mickey taken out of me just became the norm, but it was mostly without malice. I just knew He was with me, although at times I shed a lonely tear. Overall, life at sea, in the middle of the Pacific, no longer seasick, enjoying the sunshine and the companionship of workmates, was not too bad. However, long voyages at sea started to make a lot of sailors moody and fed-up. Fights broke out, but then somehow things would settle down again. These times allowed us to steer the ship, two hours at a time at the wheel. Some attempt was made to teach us navigation but very little. The first mate, whose task it was, was not a very welcoming sort of person and kept himself very much to himself. It was the second mate's job to look after the health of the crew, including jabs for various diseases. As for the captain, by now he kept himself hidden away in his cabin. On reflection, he must have been in his forties and somehow didn't fit in with life on a dirty old tramp ship.

One grey morning, *Titanbank*, our rusty wartime ship, tied up alongside in Port Chalmers, the main port of the city of Dunedin, the Edinburgh of the south, and the deep water port for the area of Otago. This part of New Zealand, especially in 1956, was very proud of its Scottish ancestry, and bagpipes and parades were common. I believe the port got its name from a Presbyterian minister. Picture a one berth wharf and a few cranes. On leaving the ship, the only sign of life was a Victorian row of drab terraced houses and a few shops at the top of the hill. The road was well-named – Grey Street. To indicate how small this port was, a shore link lived at number 29, telephone number 83.

Otago is sheep country, and so the port would mainly export wool and frozen lamb. Nothing much ever happened in Port Chalmers, but things were to change with our arrival.

I can still see the captain leaning out from the bridge, as he watched the whole crew, deck and engine-room, leaving the ship, shouting and cursing and leaving no one to run the auxiliary machinery. "We're off to get some f***ing breakfast!" The master had no choice but to give the order to shut down as the crew walked off.

To say this was entertainment for this small port would be an understatement. It was very funny, and after a couple of hours the crew began to return, already drunk, led, of course, by the dangerous chippy, liberally decorated with several strings of sausages around his neck. On seeing the captain appear again on the bridge wing, the chippy invited him to, "Stuff the sausages up your ****!" Some twelve hours later, enough crew members had returned to ensure the ship was able to run safely. The crew members were fined, discharge books stamped 'bad conduct', and the captain retreated to his cabin with his .45 revolver – 'just in case'.

Whilst writing, I decided to Google Earth Port Chalmers and wow, what a change. Grey Street remains – no terraced houses, but beautiful lawns, hedges, trees and modern Kiwi homes. Number 29 is set back, with lush vegetation on either side.

One highlight of my stay here was a short rail journey from Port Chalmers to Dunedin. The train reminded me of the Wild West films: steam, wooden seats, open ends. For journeys beyond Dunedin, one could hire a pillow for one shilling. At the various stops, passengers wanting refreshments would dash off the train, grab a coffee and return, before the ear-splitting whistle signalled departure. For a Londoner brought up with the London Underground that was hailed as the finest in the world, it was very rustic – but fun.

Dunedin was surrounded by hills, and the best way to view it was by car, at night. As I remember, the car, belonging to some Baptist folk I met there, was a 2000 Rover – very luxurious for New Zealand.

Our discharge completed, *Titanbank* steamed out of Otago Bay, and once clear of the coast, set a course for Nauru – that favourite Bank Line rendezvous. No doubt the fine Scottish folk of South Island heaved a sigh of relief.

On arrival at Nauru, we found another ship loading on the buoys. The engines were put on STOP, and the ship slowly drifted away from the island on the equatorial current. Whilst waiting, a bored crew decided to fish for sharks. Large chunks of meat on meat hooks were raided from the ship's store and attached to a wire strop (wire, so that it couldn't be bitten through). This in turn was tied to a heaving line, then through a lifeboat davit onto a steam winch. It didn't take long. The bait was flapped up and down on the surface of the water and, within minutes, a number of sharks appeared, racing back and forth, until one made for the kill, turning over on its back to grab the bait. Eager crew members, shouting and whooping, heaved on the line, and the shark was hooked and heaved from the sea, using the winch. And there it was – probably about six feet long, thrashing about on the deck with crew members trying to jump out of the way. It was still very much alive, but how to kill it? No one seemed to know. Up came our rather nasty chippy, trademark maul over his shoulder, but the blows from the maul simply bounced off the shark's skin. By this time the shark was less active, and a few brave guys tried to join in with knives. Again, these bounced off. Eventually, one of the sailors, a fisherman from Cornwall, showed he knew what to do. Out came his knife, and the shark was swiftly finished off with a knife plunged into its stomach, slitting it wide open. A very gory ending! Most of the shark was thrown back into the sea, and for a few moments the waters boiled and then – nothing. The teeth were a prize. Soon afterwards, orders came to approach the buoys.

The island was well below the horizon by now and I can remember wondering how on earth we were going to find it. Our radar was very poor, but in later years I would learn the art of navigation, which I came to love. The sun shone in a cloudless sky, 'sights' were taken, and our noon fix plus dead-reckoning of our drift soon established our position. Soon we were under the cantilever, tied up to huge buoys fore and aft, with thousands of tons of phosphate pouring into the holds. Care had to be taken of the vessel's trim, and of course, the Plimsoll lines midships on both port and starboard side watched to ensure the ship did not overload, thereby creating a possible risk of sinking.

On one of these brief visits to Nauru I managed a quick dash to the tiny harbour on the phosphate company's launch. The temperature was well into the 30 degrees C, but swimming was not recommended, as sharks and barracuda frequented the area, but just to get off the ship for a couple of hours was a relief. The small square harbour contained the rusty remains of Japanese launches – a reminder that Nauru had been taken by the Japanese in World War Two when they had taken all of this part of the Pacific, right down to the bombing of Darwin. An abiding image is of two islanders on bikes, carrying a large fish suspended on a pole between them.

Our next destination was Melbourne. A glance at a map or chart of the area will show hundreds of islands and reefs to be avoided on this journey, almost due south. I've always been taken with the name Solomon Islands. The voyage was as sea voyages are: cleaning, painting, regreasing blocks and tackle, chipping and looking forward to our landfall and, of course, Melbourne and fellowship, Christian friends, home-cooking and mail. Mail took on a mammoth importance and, should there be a scented page or envelope, homesickness would creep back in.

The landfall of the south-east Australian coast and the possible graveyard of the Bass Strait soon gave way to actually arriving at Port Phillip Bay and picking up the Melbourne pilot. The bosun was ordered to put the derricks up and make sure they were secure. Before that a number of ballast tanks (used for trim and ballast when the ship was 'light') and freshwater tanks were discharged. So, did that mean the ship had been over her Plimsoll marks and therefore overloaded when we'd left Nauru? However, things were to change; we were ordered to Adelaide instead of Melbourne, so the pilot disembarked and our course was set for Adelaide.

You could say all hell would soon let loose. The weather worsened rapidly from the south; severe storm winds directly from the Antarctic rolled in and here we were in the notorious Bass Strait. Huge waves broke over the ship – just the tops hit us. One hit the port wing of the bridge, which was now V-shaped; a port-side lifeboat disappeared, the davits bent double, while the sound of the wind screaming in the rigging added to the fear. Would the derricks, which had already been raised in readiness for cargo discharge, hold firm? If they broke free, the ship's stability would be compromised – we were already overloaded and fast running out of drinking water. As previously mentioned, the wartime SAM boats built in the USA had a reputation of breaking in half and with 10,000 tons of phosphate in her, would she hold out? She did, and eventually came alongside at Adelaide to be greeted by a bevy of newspaper reporters, eager to record our experience, which was dutifully splashed across the local newspapers. I'm pretty sure questions were asked with respect to the ship's draught, but how far this was taken I don't know.

I was looking forward to meeting up with a former girlfriend from Muswell Hill, North London. Judy McClean had married John and they'd emigrated to Australia, where John took over as manager of a garage. Judy and her sister Margaret were well known to my mum and dad, having been being part of my home church. John's aim was to work hard and eventually take over ownership of a garage in Adelaide. They lent me an old Ford Prefect to get me back to the ship. Mind you, I had no licence and you had to hold the gearstick in place or it jumped out into neutral. Still, it was great to see old friends.

Discharging bulk cargoes was always a messy business, phosphate being no exception. Of course, it was the apprentices who were sent down into the holds to begin the big clean-up. I managed to get a piece of grit in my eye, and the doctor I saw scratched my eye in the course of his examination. The shore link in Adelaide was a Mrs Derbyshire, known to all as Nanna. I had been invited to have dinner with her, and her daughter came to the dock to pick me up, took me home and decided to bandage the other eye 'for comfort'. So there was I, bandaged to the hilt. It was painful, but very funny, as the lovely Judith, Mrs Derbyshire's granddaughter, who was also a nurse, arrived and there was I without any idea what she looked like. And me a sailor! I managed a number of visits to their Baptist church where the young people were studying C. S. Lewis's *The Screwtape Letters*. The last I heard of Judith she was in Port Lincoln and now a nursing sister (retired).

Orders were received to return to Nauru, discharge at Geelong, and load grain for India, but not before loading sacks of grain, rather than bulk, from a tiny port, Ceduna, on the edge of the Great Australian Bight, where there was just a simple wooden wharf. Most of the wharfies were Aborigines, and to our great surprise, just as they were getting down to work, a shout went up from the shoreside, "The fish are in!" and off they all went to fish.

Once again our destination was Calcutta, but to our great relief the white crew was paid off and an Indian lascar crew signed on.

Our cargo for South America (Buenos Aires) was the usual – 'gunnies', also Bata shoes for Colombo, which would take up quite a bit of tween deck space. With a new crew and the Hooghly pilot on board, the captain relaxed. We subsequently learnt from the shipping agent that many of the old crew caused mayhem in a local hotel whilst waiting to return to the UK.

Titanbank carried on ploughing the seas on the usual tramp routes: Australia for grain and phosphate; India for gunnies; Africa for sisal; Brazil – iron ore for Antwerp; and cashew nuts for Cochin, India. On one occasion we spent a number of weeks in Zanzibar, an island off the east coast of Africa. We were to load a full load of scrap metal for Japan. A mad Polish diver (that was the reputation he had earnt for himself) was cutting up old World War Two ship hulks still remaining in the harbour. It was a long process and a long voyage to Japan, but eventually we offloaded the scrap in Japan; scrap metal was a major part of their growing ship-building programme. It was fascinating to see the women divers. If a piece of scrap fell into the dock on the waterside, it was the women who raced to the spot with a line attached, diving to the bottom to retrieve the scrap. Of course, the women there were also renowned as pearl divers. Then we'd sail as a 'light' ship from Japan to Nauru for phosphate, and back to Australia.

One of our voyages from India was from a port many miles inland. We simply arrived at Khalna, where there were just a few huts, tied up to buoys, and waited for the 'floating warehouses' to tie up alongside. Their cargo was once again 'gunnies' bound for South America.

Once loaded we made our way downstream for Calcutta, this time to complete the gunnie load, but also to load Bata shoes made in India. This cargo was loaded in No. 3 tween deck, then on to Colombo to complete our cargo with tea and desiccated coconut. More bunkers and water which would take us to Durban, and then on our way to Buenos Aires.

Colombo, the major port for Ceylon, was only a couple of days distance from Calcutta, and there we were to complete our cargo, before going to bunker once again in Cape Town and then Buenos Aires.

But more drama lay ahead on our arrival at Colombo.

The third mate took to his bunk with severe stomach pains, claiming the first mate had poisoned him, and was taken ashore and hospitalised on arrival. As apprentices it wasn't wise to take sides. No longer under a white crew bosun, our immediate boss was the first mate. No doubt about it – he was decidedly drunk and talked about a passenger ship in port going to Aussie: "Much better to live there!" When No. 3 hold was uncovered, about half the cargo of Bata shoes was found to be missing. Was this anything to do with the first mate who was clutching a fistful of Indian rupees? We soon learnt that the first mate had jumped ship – unheard of for a first officer! Did he manage to catch that ship to Australia? Who knows.

Cargo completed, the ship sailed and I, as senior apprentice by now, was promoted to acting third mate, which meant that I was now a watch keeper, standing on the 8-12 shift (or watch, as it was known), but at this stage I wasn't fully responsible for the ship, but standing in for the captain who was still officially in charge and available to take over, if called.

On arrival in Cape Town, the captain was reprimanded and sent home for sailing with only one suitably qualified officer; rules required a ship to have a chief officer with a master's ticket before going to sea, in case the captain should at any time be rendered out of action. Our second mate had only a second mate's qualification and I, as acting third, had nothing. I couldn't help feeling sorry for the captain, as he thought he was doing the owners a favour by getting the ship to sea and earning them money. A new captain and chief officer were duly signed on.

The negative side of my promotion was that the company kept the ship at sea for another year. This was pretty tough spiritually, but once again Father God kept me and I was so blessed by meeting Christian missionaries in a number of countries; encouraged and spoilt. There was fellowship with wonderful young people in Calcutta, Australia, New Zealand and South Africa. Then there was a little old man – a port worker I met in Visakhapatnam, who invited me to his home – what appeared to be a simple mud hut, not far from what was to become a major shipping port on the east coast of the Bay of Bengal. He was obviously very poor, but oh how he loved the Lord! I so enjoyed the diversity of all these and others I met on my travels, and still do. However, some places around docks can be dangerous, and taxi drivers couldn't always be trusted. I just committed it all to the Lord.

Eventually *Titanbank* returned to the UK. We berthed in Cardiff, the voyage having lasted ten days short of two years and two months. Except for a five week leave after *Sheilbank*, I had been continuously at sea for three years and eight months. However, I now had enough sea time to study for and sit the exams for my second mate's ticket.

Chapter 6

Man Overboard!
(And Other Adventures)

Although these precious oasis experiences fed me, as a Christian I was still very lonely. The values I had been raised with were almost completely smashed. Crews entertained girls in port. At such times I hid, struggling with my burgeoning sexual awareness, with no one to talk things through. Because of my Christian life I was mocked from time to time, but overall respected. Returning home I was viewed as something of a hero (romantic ideas!) but most blokes of my age were away on National Service or even married, in a couple of cases, leaving me even more lonely as I tried to pick up the threads. My home church hadn't a clue how to help, and the scars still remained from an encounter with the youth leader who told me that the reason I had never sailed with another Christian was because I had obviously not 'witnessed' to my fellow seamen! So I learnt to be one person at home and another at sea. Layers began to cover my naturally sensitive and tender heart. In order to keep going I would have to toughen up. And then I really fell in love. She was a young lady who worked in one of the coffee bars in Muswell Hill. She felt the same, but she was not a Christian. To a church like mine this was a serious departure from clear teaching of Scripture. I loved Scripture, but I also loved Sheila. By this time I had passed my second mate's ticket and could therefore officially be third mate. Then one morning the dreaded brown envelope fell through the letterbox. Here we go again:

> PLEASE REPORT TO THE DARTBANK AT PRESENT AWAITING A CARGO OF GERMAN COKE FOR CHITTAGONG, EAST PAKISTAN (now Bangladesh) IN ZEEBRUGGE, BELGIUM.

It was January. We'd just celebrated Christmas and New Year. How could I possibly leave? But somehow I had this deep drive within me. *I will become a master mariner*. I was told the *Dartbank* was on her maiden voyage (what a difference from the wartime ships!), with a commodore master (the senior master in the company) and a chief engineer, and we'd be home within six months.

Saying goodbye to Sheila was agony, but finally I found the strength to leave her house at the bottom of Muswell Hill and walk the three to four miles home. Snow and ice lay thick on the roads, but I made it, and the next day began my journey to Harwich where I would take the ferry to the Hook of Holland and then, from there, the train to Zeebrugge. Because of the bad weather, the ferry was hours late. All ferry buildings were closed. I looked around and found an old railway cabin on the dockside, so went in to get some shelter from the worst of the weather, and huddled there feeling very miserable. Why I didn't find a hotel in Harwich I'll never know, but I didn't. However, some hours later the ferry arrived. At last I had a warm cabin and some food, slept like a log and was eating breakfast as we approached the Hook.

Dartbank, my third ship, had come straight from sea trials and had been built in the famous Harland & Wolff yard, Belfast. What a change! A radar that worked, a modern echo-sounder and a gyro compass – everything new and shiny, as was my first gold stripe, as third officer. Zeebrugge was flat and boring with little to keep us in good spirits. I do remember that the local cinema was very modern with potted plants on either side. Some of the officers had wives and families on board to say goodbye which made me feel even worse. Eventually the coke arrived by rail from Germany and the pristine ship was soon covered with grey/black dust. It didn't take long before we slipped our moorings and, without mishap, made our way through the Dover Straits and past the Royal Sovereign Light Vessel which, incidentally, I see most days now, seven miles off Cooden Beach where we live, although the Light Vessel's former crew of three or four has now been replaced with a light platform which doubles as a helicopter platform.

Famous landmarks such as the Finisterre Light and the Rock of Gibraltar heralded our voyage into the Med and the Suez Canal. Suez is interesting, especially the narrow cut that northbound shipping passes through whilst southbound traffic waits until the canal is clear, although it looks as if the passing ships are travelling through the desert. And so to the Red Sea – as blue as blue. I doubt if many folk can say they had their 21st birthday in the Red Sea. Captain Holbrook, the commodore master, called me to his cabin, congratulated me and presented me with a can of beer. As all Bank Line ships were dry at this time – wow! That was quite something. I really enjoyed the modern 'working' navigational aids and taking sights with the second mate – a canny Scot and great. To Aden for bunkers, top up in Colombo, and finally our destination, Chittagong, an absolute hole of a place which was, in some ways, to change my life.

We tied up to buoys fore and aft about 20 yards from the riverbank. The current was swift, the moorings needing to be frequently checked, and of course it was hot and smelly. In 1958 there were hardly any buildings other than the warehouses holding the gunnies that were our next cargo for South America. An Anglican vicar dropped by – he must have been a missionary – and invited us to visit a small hall where we could buy some food 'eggs, fried sunny side up', an expression I'd never come across. An Irish ship was moored astern of us and our Irish 'sparks' went off to meet some fellow countrymen. He returned with an invitation to play hurling in an open field not far from the ships. Amazing! Playing hurling (or trying to) in East Pakistan with a group of mad Irishmen was quite a novelty, and absolutely great.

The coke was safely discharged, holds cleaned out by what seemed like hundreds of locals, and the business of loading the bales of cloth commenced. Ports in this part of the world always worked through the night, and yours truly drew the short straw as duty officer, 2000 to 0600 – a long haul. Working five hatches simultaneously, it was a lot to keep an eye on. One night I had a visit from the fourth engineer who was duty engineer and had come on deck for some cooler air. He did seem rather strange. Previous conversations with him always came back to the question of whether I liked him. He drew attention to a scar on his nose, telling me his father had hit him with a golf club, although his broad Scottish accent did make it rather difficult to understand him. But here we were, at about

0200hrs, going through all this stuff, whilst at the same time I was trying to concentrate on checking the loading at No. 1 hatch near the bow. Finally, Jock decided it was time to return to the engine room. To me, something didn't seem quite right. Looking aft, he'd disappeared. Somehow, I just knew he had jumped over the side but, without evidence, disturbing the second engineer or chief officer was a bit scary. I rushed aft and was making my way to the gangway when his voice came from the shore: "It's all right, third mate, I'm on the riverbank." He was lucky. The river was running fast on a full flood tide, but now I could call others to help. A native boatman picked him up and returned him to the ship. Second mates on tramp ships are designated ship's doctor, so the bedraggled engineer was sedated and returned to his cabin.

The story unfolded further over the next couple of weeks, as his condition deteriorated. A Pakistani doctor returning to the UK was able to escort Jock on the journey home, but until then I was ordered to stay with him in his cabin for his last day. It was touch and go: at times he seemed okay, but then his mental health condition would kick in, and it was very difficult keeping him calm. We later heard that on his arrival in the UK he caused such mayhem in a hospital ward that he had to be transferred to a secure unit. For some reason, still unknown to me, I was the next person to become the focus of attention.

Ships' logs are kept 24/7, whether in port or at sea. As duty third mate, since it was just after midnight and cargo was progressing okay, it was time for me to update the log and start the new day. I was in the officers' smoke room with the ship's 'sparks' (the crazy Irishman who'd got us all playing hurling), when the door opened and in staggered the chief engineer, very much the worse for drink. He and the master had had to be picked up from the riverbank, dead drunk, and heaved up the gangway and into their cabins. So much for being the commodore master and chief engineer! Anyway, I became the chief's target. He decided I needed to be taught a lesson and grabbed hold of me, trying to hit me, cursing and swearing. He may have been in his sixties, but was still very strong; I was twenty-one and skinny, but fortunately strong enough to hold him off.

I don't know what came over me, but I promptly decided and announced that I was going to enter a formal complaint with the company, and to sue him on our return to the UK. I had witnesses, and also got the chief officer out of his bunk as a witness. I can remember being very shaken, but something in me seemed to rise up: *Right, I've had enough of this*, I vowed. *In future, I'll make sure I get at the other person before he gets to me.* Little did I know that this vow and a new aggressive attitude towards people would become very much part of the persona I was developing. It wasn't until 2001, with Ellel Ministries (more later), that I came to understand how this event affected the problems I was storing up, and how renouncing this, a sinful vow, led to forgiveness and healing. Was Father still with me? Yes, of course He was, but lack of fellowship again, another hostile captain, and wanting to be with Sheila, all began to rob me of my walk with the Lord.

Our cargo was complete and *Dartbank* was bound for Buenos Aires, calling in at Cape Town for bunkers. On arrival, Captain Holbrook called me to his cabin: would I be willing to forget the whole incident in exchange for transferring to the *Ettrickbank* (currently in port there) as second mate? I jumped at the chance of getting off what was for me a very unhappy ship, plus the added bonus of promotion. What I didn't quite grasp was that the *Ettrickbank* was one of two vessels trading on what was known as the Oriental/African line – all ports between Cape Town and Tokyo and back. By the time I actually transferred to the *Ettrickbank*, almost another six months had passed and, whereas after Buenos Aires the *Dartbank* would be returning to the UK, it was to be another eighteen months before I, now on the *Ettrickbank*, could legally pay off in Singapore and return home.

Second mates are responsible for navigation, cargo plans, ship's health (acting as doctor) and of course the very tiring 'graveyard' watch. My first job was to plot the courses for the East African part of the journey. Did I have all the necessary charts? Were they up to date? Notices to mariners were produced on a monthly basis, I think, or at least when necessary, so chart correction took a number of hours. I well remember drawing and inking in the new Hong Kong airport which ran right into the sea.

Well, *Ettrickbank* was very different from the *Dartbank*. Built in 1937 (my birth year), it had a radar that didn't really work, an echo-sounder which just about did, and two old magnetic compasses – one in the wheelhouse and one on the monkey island. The master, Captain Williams, was usually 'well-oiled' but a great navigator who fired my love for navigation. He came from a long line of Irish shipbuilders and, to pass the time, would build dinghies from the timber cargoes, with the help of the Chinese chippy.

My first voyage as second mate was memorable, leaving Cape Town on my watch, 0000 to 0400, in rough weather. The Cape is notorious for big seas and rounding the Cape meant hanging on for dear life or being thrown from one side of the wheelhouse to the other. We'd loaded a varied general cargo. A weak counter current ran up the coast towards the equator and Captain Williams took full advantage of this – at times a few hundred yards off the beach. In some places it was so shallow we could see the bottom of the sea. I grew to love the risks as well as the skill. Even in mid Indian Ocean the captain's arrival on the bridge for noon 'sights' would promote a few degrees of a change of course which would make all the difference. All oceans have ocean current maps: thousands of small arrows indicate a current which is the movement of water caused by the high and low pressure systems of the oceans, the meeting of cold with warm water, added to which is the drift of water being blown in the direction of wind.

(Let me briefly highlight the difference between sailing with the likes of Captain Williams and Bank Line and other shipping companies. A few years after this, I was to join Shaw Savill on fast, refrigerated cargo ships to Australia and New Zealand, from which one hardly ever saw the coast, unless approaching port, keeping 20 to 50 miles off land. Not much in the way of coastal navigation needed there, whereas this was part and parcel of Captain William's skills, although it could be a bit risky at times. However, with Shaw Savill ships I felt I was no longer a navigator; it was simply a matter of radar and gyro compass – all very helpful, but not the same.)

Back to my first voyage as second mate. It took six weeks to load cargo on the South and East African coast, calling at Cape Town, Port Elizabeth, East London and Durban, then Lourenco Marques (now Maputo), Beira, Tanga, Matara, Dar-es-Salaam, Zanzibar and Mombasa. One memory of Mombasa has remained: the ship had almost completed loading and as second mate I was responsible for drawing up all the cargo manifests, meaning a hatch plan for all five holds – the right cargo in the right hold, what was there and its tonnage. These were mailed to ports of discharge and therefore, which cargo was where, how much and of course all in the right order, was vital. The loading of No. 1 hold was almost finished, and the pipe-smoking shoreside cargo manager, with a great Voortrekker moustache and Afrikaner hat, perched on the hatch, and in general conversation with me about the way African nations and indeed nations throughout the whole world were now changing remarked, "I would never have believed that I would see the break-up of the British Empire in my lifetime." And so we left for the Far East, course north-east across the Indian Ocean, towards the northern tip of Sumatra and the Malacca Straits, on our way to Singapore.

In the north-east monsoon the Indian Ocean is mostly a calm and beautiful sea – mile after mile of stunning sunrises and sunsets, wonderful skies, millions of stars. I learnt my stars – particularly the ones used for navigation – with the aid of my 4s 6d copy of *Bernard's Nautical Star Chart* spread out on the chart table. Obviously latitude limited my sight of many when in the northern hemisphere and likewise when in the south. Our course from Mombasa was almost parallel to the equator as we crossed into the northern hemisphere, and then altered course to round the north-west point of Sumatra. I remember having to wear sunglasses because of the glare of a full moon right ahead, making it difficult to see. Watches consisted of the duty officer (me), and three seamen, one on lookout on the fo'c'sle head (no autohelm), another steering the ship, and one on standby. Sleep became a problem. The 0000-0004 watch was punishing: up before midnight, four hours' watch and trusting the mate would arrive at 0400, then often back on the bridge at 0730 to 0800 for a.m. sun sight-taking with the third mate. Usually, after breakfast at 0830, the second mate (now me) would, as ship's doctor, hold the daily clinic, followed, maybe, by a bit of personal time before noon sights, then watch duty until 1600, dinner at 1800 and hopefully to your bunk for 1900, before starting it all over again on the 0000-0004 watch. My constant fear was of falling asleep on watch: 0200, ship gently pitching and rolling, moon ahead and *bang*! How come I'm on the deck? I spent much of the time mentally telling myself not to fall down the ladder from the bridge wing, on to the deck below.

The Indian Ocean is also subject to the south-west monsoon. The north-east monsoon blows cold air from off the Himalayas, which is dry; the south-west monsoon blows across the Indian Ocean, picking up moisture, hence huge amounts of rain, not only at sea but also over the South East Asian continent, resulting in constant rain, high humidity, hot and unpleasant with winds varying from force 3 to 6 or 7 on the Beaufort scale.

One scary incident on the 12-4 shift sticks in my memory: we were in a south-west monsoon, with heavy rain, rough seas and poor visibility. I was expecting to pick up the lighthouse on the north-west tip of Sumatra – no radar, just good eyesight. Yes – there it was, just about showing through the rain and cloud – but no, it's gone – yes – there it is again, up to the monkey island to take an azimuth bearing. Little or no difference from the previous one. Five minutes later still no change, which meant that we were heading straight for it. Urgent call to the master. A radical change of course to port righted us until the light was well on the starboard quarter, then another change of course. The light now showed we were now well clear of the rocks as we entered the Straits of Malacca, a very busy shipping lane, with ships from Singapore and the Far East making their way to the Indian Ocean. At other times, due to atmospheric conditions and the heat of the day, ships appearing on the horizon would seem to be upside down, as a result of refraction.

Our next destination was Singapore. The *Ettrickbank*'s crew were all Chinese, except for officers. Singapore had been a British outpost during the Second World War and was still recovering from the Japanese invasion. It became a republic in 1963 and a sovereign nation in 1965 and is now a tightly controlled global trading nation and very clean, but in 1958 Singapore was still a shabby place and famous among seafarers for its nightlife.

Our stay wasn't to be long – simply oil bunkers and some cargo. We were fully loaded from the African coast, bound for Hong Kong, South Korea and Japanese ports. We tied up to buoys in the outer harbour and most of the officers went ashore. Just after midnight it was time to leave. The pilot was aboard and I was down aft, supervising the 'letting go' of the ship. It was my watch and it was going to be a bit tough navigating through the Straits of Singapore. The pilot was still aboard when I arrived on the bridge. He was very concerned, asking me if I wanted the ship returned to the buoys as the master was drunk, the first mate was drunk and the third mate had escaped to his cabin. I decided that the problems of explaining the escalating port costs to Captain Williams would be greater than having a go at navigating the Straits by myself. The pilot disembarked and I picked out the buoyed channel.

As second mate navigation was my responsibility, but the Straits were renowned for shipping as well as for dhows which were a law unto themselves – one actually bounced down the side of the ship! To make matters worse, both the radar and the echo-sounder broke down. I felt really tense; at first there were plenty of light buoys to guide us, but these became fewer as we steamed for the position two miles off the Brothers (a small group of islands), well marked by a lighthouse. Once there I squared away north-north-east for Hong Kong, via Saigon, in French Indochina.

I began to wonder if a cigarette would relieve the tension. A tin of cigarettes with matches had been left in the chartroom, so I decided to give it a go. Once over the dizzy spell it felt really good. And so I started smoking – initially the odd one but, as cigarettes were 10s 6d for 200 in tins of 50, it was easy to quickly build up a habit of 20 to 30 a day. I was now a smoker and in much of the Christian world this was a sin. It was these thoughts that gradually caused me to lose heart. I had had little fellowship of any depth for many months and felt lonely and isolated. Having passed the Brothers safely I was now expecting to be relieved on watch by the mate who failed to show up. However, at 0500 the captain staggered onto the bridge in a panic, wanting to know where we were. I politely showed him, bade him good morning and left the bridge.

I was very tired having worked most of the previous day, stood my watch and that of most of the first mate's, and would in any case be required to be back on the bridge by 0800 to check the ship's position and 'take sights' with the third mate. Was it then that I decided to have a drink? 8s 6d for a bottle of whisky; 18 shillings for 24 beers. I soon discovered that beer sent me to sleep with a headache, whereas whisky gave me a kick. It had been about a year since I'd seen home, church and Sheila, with still another year to go. I was now smoking and drinking (not much), and forgetting who I was in Christ. The magic of Japan lay before me, with enticing, pretty girls all around. It wasn't a particularly horrible thought – in fact, it held rather nice possibilities.

This voyage turned out to be dramatic in more ways than one. The Vietnam War was still to come, and our stay in Saigon only lasted a couple of days, leaving a brief assortment of memories. Pre-war tensions were building, but the city seemed to be calm enough, though crowded and very busy. Once again we made it safely back to the ship.

That evening the first mate took me out to a top restaurant; he'd been given a large sum of money that I guess was probably a bribe of some sort. Sadly, in those days I was fearful of being sick and therefore wary of eating foreign food, so I ate very little. What on earth the first mate thought of me I have no idea. We sailed the next day, and not long afterwards the French lost Indochina, but only after the Americans stepped in, making it a very bloody conflict.

The shortest way to Hong Kong was through the Formosa Straits (Formosa is now Taiwan). The nationalist Chinese were battling it out with the communists, so we went outside of Formosa by way of the South China Sea and were dramatically buzzed by USA light aircraft and then by two national Chinese destroyers; one crossed the bow and the other raced up the port side with guns trained on us, as they demanded to know who we were and where we were bound. I can remember almost dying of laughter to see the 'Old Man' jumping up and down on the bridge like a maniac, shouting, "If they fire I'll stop!" No more excitement as we steamed into Hong Kong.

Our stay in Hong Kong was merely to change crew, so a few hours later we slipped our moorings and headed for Inchon, South Korea. My duty station over, I went to my cabin. The bunk was absolutely covered with bottles of booze – mine with two layers, the first mate's with three and the third mate's a mere one.

The Chinese are big gamblers and smugglers, and the truth of this we were to discover in Inchon. It wasn't long before we officers realised that our 'boy' or steward wasn't quite what we thought he was and couldn't even make a bunk. The chief steward also seemed to be a little strange and no wonder. Almost before we dropped anchor, swarms of customs officers came aboard. The chief steward and other stewards were handcuffed and taken off the ship.

Apparently, the customs officers had been waiting for a long time to capture this gang of smugglers. Watches, cameras and all sorts of other contraband were concealed amongst the stores. We were ordered to discharge our cargo for Inchon – a few hundred tons of pitch donated by the USA Government – and then escorted to an anchorage to await clearance to leave.

The ship's stewards were arrested and our length of stay seemed as if it could be days or months, but a couple of days later, Captain Williams made his bold escape. As luck would have it, the venture happened on my watch. The ship was put on standby. Everything was ready: plenty of power to raise the anchor; lifeboats ready; crew on standby and lookouts placed, but no steaming lights – in fact, no lights at all! As I've said before, Williams was a superb seaman.

Our night time escape route necessarily took us between a number of small islands. I guess the radar must have been working for a change, and after what seemed to be a very long time, we crept out into the Yellow Sea, steaming south outside of South Korea's national waters to the south-west point of Korea, then squaring away for a small port called Moji on the west coast of Japan's southern island, Kyushu.

Chapter 7
In the Eye of the Typhoon

Moji lies on the northern tip of Kyushu, a narrow strait that separates Kyushu from the much bigger island of Honshu and Japan's Inland Sea. In Moji we were met by the famous Moji Mary – a lady who had been selling Japanese goods to seafarers for many years. I remember buying a pair of binoculars for £5 – not a bad price for 8 x 50 magnification. I had with me a photograph of me in uniform, taken on my last leave back home when I was twenty-one, and this was projected on to a piece of silk cloth before being hand-painted for framing, as a gift for my mum. I found this rather embarrassing as I was told I looked like the young Duke of Edinburgh. I also bought and still have a tea set of very small, fine china which, when the cup was emptied and held up to the light, revealed the face of a geisha girl in the base. I expect the Japanese made millions of these for tourists. I think it cost me something like £3 to £5 and is currently up in the attic.

Our stay here was very brief. I was looking forward to Osaka, but first we had to navigate the Inland Sea. In the late 1950s a buoyed channel directed shipping into the ports of Osaka and Kobe. The navigation chart showed hatching on either side of the channel, indicating areas where mines had been laid down during the war. It was one of the second mate's jobs to update charts from the monthly document *Notices to Mariners* that was sent throughout the world. It was still not unusual for mines to be spotted or trawled up by fishermen.

Part of our cargo was discharged at Osaka where I spent one of the most uncomfortable church services I was ever to experience. I left the ship, hailed a 10 yen taxi (1000 yen to the pound), and directed the driver to 1565 Sumiyoshi Cho, Abenoku, Osaka, the home of a Mr and Mrs Budd, British missionaries who were the local shore links. This was real, authentic Japanese housing – a small wooden building tucked in amongst many similar structures. Number 1565? Or was that the district? Knock on the door, shoes off, and the joy of meeting this lovely Christian couple and, being Sunday, off to church, yet again a little wooden hut with about twenty present, and no seats, only cushions.

Our stay didn't last long. A short passage to Kobe then on to Nagoya and Yokahama. Despite my very welcome meeting with the Budds, the time away from home (now over a year), plus my grief at what turned out to be losing Sheila, began to drain me – spirit, soul and body. I was tired. The 0000-0400 watch, also known as the 'graveyard watch', was taking its toll; all Far East ports worked 24 hours with no let-up. My Bible reading became a thing of the past, and prayer was like talking into a vast empty space, and yet not empty at all – it was full of pretty Japanese girls, bright lights and very erotic Japanese art.

Ashore in Japan was, in some ways, a nightmare. One could hardly move for pimps and girls and bars. In Kobe an enterprising South African had set up a bar named after good old Blighty – Ye Olde Kings Arms. To my knowledge it was the only place in Japan where there were no girls, but everything that could be moved, such as beer mats, cruets, cutlery etc, bore the inscription 'This was stolen from Ye Olde King's Arms' and it was a matter of honour to come away with at least one item.

On one venture ashore a particular bar seemed to be empty. Could this be a place of respite for a quick meal and drink? It was still not long after the war and the Japanese were allowed to build naval ships, but without any guns, and they were bitter at this perceived humiliation. The Yanks were still largely in control of the Japanese docks and shipping and I think most, if not all of the ports, were patrolled by USA marine police. As Brits, we were popular and much in demand to help with English. Ports were divided into two zones – clean and unclean (venereal disease) – and certain areas were strictly out of bounds to USA naval crews, hence the military police.

Back to the bar – no pimps, no girls, so in we went. Within minutes a bunch of drunken American seamen staggered in and, approaching the bar lady, proceeded to give graphic descriptions of the size and shape of girls they were looking for. It was hilarious.

One of the men came over to me looking very worried; apparently, I looked like one of the officers, which would have meant he was in big trouble, but then the situation got even worse for them as a couple of military policemen walked in. A couple of us were in the toilet when two Yanks burst in, looking for a way to escape. In desperation they ripped out the small bamboo window, squeezed through and fled. Had we seen any crew? "No, not a sign!" Nightlife in Kobe was fun. Before we left, a dozen girls came in following a meal break, and we beat a hasty retreat to the docks, to the roar of winches, railway carriages and the shouts and noise of working men, ships and docks.

Yokohama and Tokyo – so big, almost one city, a mass of bright lights, ships, pimps and girls. Our cargo was almost discharged and so far we had only loaded a few hundred tons of plywood for South Africa. To steam out of Yokohama with the moon shining on Mount Fuji, the most perfect volcanic cone in the world, was magical. On our portside, a small volcanic island was erupting and ahead lay the voyage to a number of exotic countries. The first, south of Japan on our long journey back to South Africa, was a small port in the Philippines, Iloilo. The city lies on one of the westerly islands of the Pacific about 11 degrees north of the equator. We were to load a few hundred tons of timber, but this voyage could well have been our last, as Typhoon Lorna was right in the way, gradually building up and becoming deadly.

A typhoon is a tropical revolving storm (TRS). These are born in hot seas, 10 degrees north or south of the equator. As the hot air above the sea expands and rises, cooler air moves in to replace this. If it rises too far, the air becomes cold and heavy, descending rapidly until warmed again, and hence a typhoon is born. Because of the rotation of the earth, the TRS also begins to rotate and begins to travel over the sea in a north-westerly direction – in the case of the northern hemisphere. It does sometimes continue in that direction but more often recurves through north to north-east. The sea is the fuel, but as soon as the storm strikes land it begins to 'fill', air pressure increases and, after creating much damage, it dies out.

A few days out from Japan weather reports began to come in telling us of a TRS forming ahead of us and due to cross the Philippines. Some reports came from the US base on Guam Island,

and planes flew as near to the centre of the typhoon as possible to take photos of radar shots. At first the storm wasn't strong enough to warrant altering course; we were heading south to south-east and steaming behind the storm. Yes, the weather would be poor. The ship had no cargo to speak of and, in seaman's terms, she was 'light', with little draught, and so the rudder and propeller were only about half under the water. In other words she would be like a heavy balloon blown by the wind.

However, Captain Williams was a good seaman. He read and considered the weather reports and the estimated barometric pressure, then made the decision to hold course, believing it was not too bad, and in any case the storm was moving away from us. Unfortunately, his decision was wrong. We found ourselves right smack bang in the middle of 'Lorna'. The strength of the wind was well over 100 miles per hour, the size and power of the waves enormous, and the rain, which can only be described as like sitting under a waterfall, left us blind. When the *Ettrickbank* pitched, her bow was buried under mountains of water, her stern came right out of the water and the engine raced. Thankfully the 'governor' (a regulator for maintaining a regular speed) cut in and reduced the revolutions of the ship's engines, thus preventing the screw from shearing off under the strain. The rudder, too, was mostly out of the water which meant steering was almost impossible. I can remember sitting on the wheel, holding on for dear life and waiting twenty agonising minutes before the ship's head responded and began to turn.

Rolling was even worse. The *Ettrickbank* was a 'flush deck' ship, meaning that the main decks had open rails rather than bulwarks. Massive waves came aboard. Being 'light' probably saved us, since if fully loaded, the weight of the water on deck could have driven us under. Would the hatch covers hold? If they didn't we would be gone in a matter of minutes.

I think I have always been a bit of a madcap so, true to form, I volunteered to go on deck with the ship's carpenter to take soundings. Dozens of sounding pipes covered the deck and the carpenter was responsible for taking soundings every day, with a weighted line, to see if any water was entering the bilges. Lifelines had been rigged, so we went on deck, clipped on and tried to achieve the impossible. Even if we managed to unscrew a sounding cap, the waves overwhelmed us, and all we could do was cling on to the lifeline for our lives.

The storm lasted a number of days. No one could sleep. We tried to keep normal watches and, like all seamen, braved it out and hoped for the best.

And then we went through the 'eye'. This is an area in the centre of a storm which is a vacuum, due to the revolving nature of storms. Suddenly it was eerily silent. The waves no longer broke as there was no wind to whip them up. It was very scary and then it hit us. As we went through the eye the strongest winds were on the edge. An incredible, unearthly scream rent the air as the wind returned, laying the ship over as if it were a toy, and once again huge waves were crashing over us. When the *Ettrickbank* pitched, her bow rose very high, then crashed down as the wave passed over and under her. We learnt later that the ship's bottom had been pushed in all the way from No. 1 hold to No. 3, where the accommodation began. Thank God for 'double bottoms'.

Perhaps my worst experience of this time was when I came on watch at midnight – up onto the funnel deck and then to the bridge. Looking around, I saw dozens of seabirds, exhausted, drenched, some dead but all sucked into the centre by the storm. Looking aft, for the first time I felt real fear: an owl, clinging on for dear life, stared up at me from the deck. An *owl*? A land bird? Where on earth were we? We had little or no idea! Yes – off the east coast of the many islands that make up the Philippines, but whereabouts? We'd had no 'sights' for days, no radar (not working, as usual) and the echo sounder, such as it was, indicated 'no bottom'.

In a way the storm saved us by moving faster than the ship through the islands, until weaker winds, lighter rain, and lower seas enabled us to begin to make some headway. I still don't know how we made landfall, or how on earth Captain Williams found the entrance between the islands which lay in front of the island port (Iloilo) that we were heading for. We now found ourselves trying to walk on an upright and steady deck, staggering from side to side, holding on to avoid falling and being sick – a common problem for some seamen after a long spell at sea – particularly in rough weather.

Having made it to my cabin, instead of lying on the cabin deck and wedging myself between the bunk and the bulkhead, as during the typhoon, I now climbed into my bunk and fell asleep.

A few hours of precious sleep were rudely interrupted by a heavy banging on my cabin door. Customs officers were insisting on searching the entire ship. All crew were allowed 200 cigarettes, one bottle of spirits and a case of beer; anything more resulted in a fine. As far as I'm aware nothing of significance was found on this particular occasion.

Because of our structural damage we were not allowed to leave port until given permission by a Lloyd's surveyor. We had taken in water, but were ordered back to Japan, Osaka, for repairs, and so Mitsubishi Dockyard was to be our home for the next couple of weeks.

Here I discovered Japan's industrial army. At 0750 sharp every morning a very loud siren blasted out over the dry dock. Within seconds, clad in baseball trousers, white T-shirts and baseball caps, the entire dock workforce *ran* out of the changing rooms (imagine that happening in the UK!); music from large loudspeakers shattered what sound space was left, and the 'army' went through five minutes of intensive exercise. At 0755 another siren blast and the 'army' raced back to the changing rooms. On the dot of 0800 – you've guessed it – another blast saw the workforce *running* to their work stations. It seemed as if only seconds had passed before the air was full of the sounds of riveting and hammering. Of course, being in dry dock meant we had to use shoreside toilets and washrooms, and we soon learnt that, in Japan, one was expected to wash oneself thoroughly *before* entering the bath – no sitting in dirty bathwater for the Japanese. Makes sense really. These times in port were bliss for those who stood the 12-4 watches: to get into one's bunk by about 10 p.m. and sleep through the night until 7 a.m. was amazing, but took quite a bit of getting used to.

It was during this time that Japan saw its first workers' strike. Taxi drivers stopped work for twenty minutes, in protest about wages and vehicle registrations, so Mitsubishi dock workers also stopped. It was obvious they didn't know quite what they were supposed to do during a strike and some were laughing, whilst others just stood and looked around nervously. Twenty minutes wasn't long but, as I learnt from talking with some of the senior dock authorities, it was very significant. Striking was a totally alien concept in the 1950s to 1960s, as Japanese workers were rebuilding their nation after the war, rebuilding their self-esteem and beginning to take control of their lives and working conditions.

I learnt a lot during our stay in dock. The first mate was rather large and couldn't get into the double bottoms, the space between the ship's hull (outer skin) and the hold bottom. I was rather skinny, so was asked to work alongside the Lloyd's surveyor, dockyard manager and ship's master.

It was a really small space, and squeezing through the ship's light holes to the area where repairs were taking place was a bit claustrophobic. A light was put down, but it was easier to use my torch, although I did worry a bit about getting lost on the way back to the entrance manhole on No. 1 hold deck. Still, it was a great experience for my mate's and master's tickets. On completion of the work, the A1 Lloyd's surveyor and the master asked me to go with the dry dock manager and check that the repairs had been completed satisfactorily. I must say I felt rather proud to be asked. The surveyor then told us that when the first cargo ship was completed by the Japanese, after the war, they had requested a Lloyd's A1 certificate, but unfortunately no non-Japanese was slim enough to be able to squeeze through the light holes to do the checks.

The ship now being A1, we could proceed to Iloilo, and this time our journey went without any tropical storms. A few tons of timber were loaded and we were off to Borneo and Sandakan. My memories of Sandakan are of a single wharf where we loaded huge hardwood logs. At that time, de-forestation had only just begun; the jungle was very near and few buildings existed. I ventured into the jungle for a few hundred yards before realising I hadn't a clue where I was, nor what to do if confronted by any wildlife. It was quite dark, so I beat a hasty retreat.

The cargo handlers were not very skilled; one winch handler allowed the drum wire to run out, sending a log crashing to the bottom of the hold so, once again, we had damage to the hold bottom. However, it was deemed to be minor so, once loading was completed we set off for our next port of call – Bangkok.

Bangkok also turned out to be somewhat eventful. We tied up to buoys in the Bangkok river to load more logs and teak squares. At that particular time Bangkok authorities would not allow Chinese nationals ashore (the crew was Chinese) but a liberty boat took us to the steps not far from the dock gates. There was a strong army presence with rifles loaded and more or less at the ready. I was with one of our South African apprentices who, like some other South Africans I had met, was very interested in firearms.

We decided to have a quick drink outside the gates, but had only just sat down when a very loud row broke out between two prostitutes and, oh boy, could they fight. Thai boxing and masses of hair pulled out. It was brutal, but more seriously our apprentice suddenly decided to get a closer look at one of the soldier's rifles. He didn't get far; up leapt the soldier, safety catch off, rifle aimed, resulting in one stupid apprentice shaking like a leaf and most of us in the café down on the ground! The incident calmed down, apologies were made, and off we went by taxi to see the famous Golden Pagoda.

The pagoda was indeed very beautiful, with ornate carvings and many strange figures painted with gold leaf. The main attraction was the huge Buddha, and I watched, almost in horror, as many crawled up to the Buddha on their knees, to place their offerings of gold leaf on the huge idol, and I was struck by the same despairing expressions worn on their faces as they crawled back. We wandered past a building, the grounds of which were full of orange-clad monks. These were 'scholars' – some very young. I was given to understand that it was an honour to send one's first-born son for such training. As we left, we couldn't help laughing as we saw that the boys standing by the door, and out of sight of the staff, were firing paper pellets at each other. I guess boys will be boys the world over!

We escaped, and behaved with exceptional care as we made our way back to the jetty and the ship.

Being moored in the Bangkok river had some advantages: it was cooler than being alongside, but also provided some amusement. Ships had dozens of pretty girls on board – all banned by the authorities. One morning, a Dutch freighter slowly made her way upriver; two Jacob's ladders were dropped from the stern, and two boats fastened to them. I have no idea how many girls tried to climb the ladders – not easy at the best of times – but the breeze clearly presented a magnificent display of bums and legs. Slowly, the ship continued upriver, with her first 'cargo' well and truly on board and safely stowed in a number of cabins. (In Nelson's Navy days a shout of "Show a leg!" would ring out and the women in the hammocks sticking out a leg would avoid being tipped out.)

Bangkok boasted a seamen's club with a swimming pool. Fantastic! To sit in a lounge, sipping a cold drink, was a real treat, but what really livened it up were our nocturnal escapades, as we climbed over the wall after the place was locked up for the night, to enjoy skinny dipping with a bunch of girls – not that we saw any nudity as it was so dark.

Our radio officer – a really nice guy – was an alcoholic whose downfall was gin. His cabin adjoined the radio shack, and you can imagine our shock and amusement on discovering that, finding the 'journey' through the door from his cabin into the radio room was just too much, he had simply cut a hole – a shortcut to it – through the wooden bulkhead! He paid off in Cape Town, but how long would it take for him to sober up? How we missed him. However, he was replaced by a sober, rather serious and much safer radio officer. Ships relied heavily on radio signals for sending vital weather info, ship's business and of course ordering those important bunches of flowers to parents and sweethearts for Christmas and birthdays etc.

Home and church were now distant memories. I remember thinking that it didn't matter any more. Sheila didn't matter. God? Well, yes, it used to be good, but somehow in a different world. My world now was ship, navigation and seamanship, staying alive and arriving in Cape Town/Durban, but friends there didn't fit any more either. It wasn't that I didn't enjoy myself: I was now confident as an officer, confident that I could navigate, confident that a ship could safely be in my sole charge for at least eight hours in twenty-four, confident that I could be 'ship's doctor'. (More of that later…)

I look back now, and can see how Father God kept and protected me all the time, but sadly, my state of mind then, plus all the other stuff, led me to finally give in when it came to 'ladies of easy virtue', but that was enough to further crush my spirit, and in any case it was a lousy experience. The shame and fear I felt guaranteed I would never enjoy that. I was never a drinker and I hated that too, loathed it. The warnings of my Christian upbringing, combined with my horror of backsliding, produced a hard lump in my chest. I hated church, Christians and God, the world and all that it stood for.

> *I tried the broken cisterns Lord*
> *But ah the waters failed*
> *And even as I stooped to drink*
> *They fled and mocked me as I wailed*
> *(J.McGranahan)*
> (This expressed my experience and feelings so well.)

In the world's eyes I had hardly done anything wrong, but in my eyes I was utterly sinful and utterly lost, but – no Church, no Christians and when I did eventually meet them (only going to church to please my mum) I was judged, talked about, criticised: "See that Mike Gale? He smokes."

And yet God had not given up on me. On one of our many Indian Ocean voyages, I came off watch on a typical afternoon of sun, blue sky and a gentle rocking swell – not too hot. I'd developed a habit of drinking whisky, a third of a pint tumbler at a time, neat. Having handed over to the first mate, I went into my cabin, poured my usual whisky, and settled down to enjoy it. At that moment the third mate came in, looked at me and simply said, "Second Mate, you're really knocking that stuff down." I stopped, looked at my glass, looked at the third mate and then looked up. I saw very clearly In front of me a country-style crossroad signpost: one arm said ALCOHOLIC, and the opposite NON-ALCOHOLIC. I felt nothing, but absolutely knew that I had to make a decision, and there and then gathered up all my whisky and other alcoholic drinks and threw them overboard. It was many years before I touched another drop.

I wonder who was praying for me at that moment. Mum? An old friend? An old Scottish shore link somewhere? Recently, I heard that the young men's group back at my home church in London, always prayed for me. Wow! I didn't know that. I wonder who is praying, or has prayed for you for many years?

Yes, my Heavenly Father was still watching over me, and when he says 'I have called you by name' (Isaiah 43:1) he means it; when he says 'I knew you in your mother's womb' (Ps139) it's true; when he says 'I have plans and purposes for you' (Jer 29:11) he does, and when, two years later, having tried to walk in front of oncoming cars, and hating myself even more because I didn't have the courage to really do it, he kept me.

But first: the duties of a second mate as ship's doctor.

Chapter 8
Ship's Doctor

Ship's doctor? *Me?* One of the responsibilities of second mate was the health of crew and officers. A second mate's ticket required a First Aid certificate. Some study was necessary, but word quickly got around that the pass fee was 10 shillings, and the doctor who was asking the questions would quickly provide the answers if the candidate hesitated!

And so it was that, with my new second mate's ticket (now six months old), I left the *Dartbank*, joined the *Ettrickbank*, and returned to the oceans, knowing full well that 'tramps' never carried doctors, and that the seat of all knowledge was the second mate who, in shipping terms, should have his mate's ticket before becoming actual second mate. Little did I appreciate that on the 1st August 1958, as second mate of the *Ettrickbank*, I would become ship's doctor.

The crew were Chinese and tiger balm was a panacea for all ills. After my 1200 to 1600 watch, crew members would come to me with a variety of ailments. A *Shipmaster's Reference Book for Diseases, Common Problems and Ills* was available – not comprehensive, but it did cover what seemed to be most eventualities. It was frightening to realise the number of serious diseases which begin with a headache and a bit of a temperature, and this resulted in many an anxious moment: was it a headache? A malingerer? Typhoid?

My first real encounter turned out to be serious. I was woken up before my usual turn-to at 0000hrs with a lot of banging and shouting; one of the crew members (we'll call him Soong) had apparently gone berserk. This particular sailor only spoke Mandarin, whilst the rest of the crew spoke Cantonese. Over the weeks since leaving Hong Kong, some of the crew had mocked and baited him. They'd messed up his kit and hidden his watch, and a few days earlier he had been found clinging to a lifeboat on the boat deck, refusing to move. We had eventually got him to move, and obviously the master was involved, talking to the crew's bosun, and we hoped the problem had been solved. But no, I was now presented with a semi-conscious engine-room worker whose head had been split open with a hammer. Soong had gone down the emergency ladder into the engine room and was now there, running amok, and could potentially do a lot of damage to the machinery, let alone other crew members. He was caught and confined in a spare cabin, with one of the apprentices appointed to look after him.

Now, what on earth to do next? Ah yes, a good idea – sedate him. The medical kit stowed in a cupboard in the officers' saloon did have some outdated ampoules of morphine which might help. How to administer it? Well, the examining doctor in Commercial Road hadn't asked me that question, but we very quickly discovered that he was so used to taking opium that nothing we had made any difference. I then managed to clean the victim's head wound, and decided that, although he needed stitches, he would probably survive with a good wound dressing. In time the wound healed well and he was later assured that everything was okay by a doctor in Bangkok.

But not so poor Soong. The apprentice guarding him needed a quick break and within seconds Soong was once again on the loose. He was found and returned to the cabin, but how could we restrain a man who, for all we knew, had lost his mind? Ships carry a special rescue stretcher, called a Neil Robertson, made of wooden slats and stout canvas. Once a person is in it, the sides are tied across, and the head and feet also securely anchored, ensuring that movement of the normally badly injured person would be restricted.

I can still feel a certain revulsion after all these years. How can one do this to another human being? Putting him into a virtual straitjacket? However, for his safety we tied him in. It took two to three days before we reached Bangkok, and Soong, considerably weaker and calmer, was escorted to hospital. At that time, the Chinese were not allowed ashore in Thailand, so Soong was taken away under escort.

The story had a good ending: nine months later the *Ettrickbank* came alongside in Hong Kong for a crew change, and there was Soong, waiting on the dock, fit and well. He had come to collect his kit and personal belongings, including his watch. It was good to see him so safe and well.

Another nasty accident – this time involving one of the engine-room greasers whose job at the time was to 'flash up' the boilers. Diesel fuel was spun, injected into the receptacle, where the fuel was fired to heat the boiler. Standard instructions were not to inject too much; if the oil fails to ignite, stop, clean out the excess fuel and start again. Well, he didn't, was caught in the way of a nasty flashback and quite badly burnt on his face and arms. The standard treatment was to apply burn dressings. I took a lot of care treating him and was gratified to be rewarded by, "Congratulations," from the doctor in Bangkok. The burns were clean and healing well by the time he saw them.

On one occasion, as we were approaching Singapore, the bosun and crew were told to raise the derricks – a simple enough job but, as with all running gear, potentially dangerous. The wire rope attached to the head of the derrick was secured by blocks to the deck by each derrick, then wound round the winch drum, lifted to an appropriate angle, then tied off. To put it simply, the wire rope on one derrick wasn't held fast before being secured, and so the derrick began to drop down, somehow catching his hand, and in particular his thumb, in the block sheave. When I saw his thumb it was like a stripped banana, with just a bone sticking out, and flesh hanging down.

Word was quickly sent to the port agents. A boat would leave immediately, and Captain Lynch ordered me to go with the bosun and make sure he arrived safely in hospital. But meanwhile, I wondered how I should a) dress the wound? and b) try to alleviate the pain?

Well, (a) was straightforward, but (b)? I'd given a lot of penicillin injections. The *Masters' Handbook* shows a bare bottom with a line from one side to the other, forming a cross: you simply stick the needle in the centre! But this was different. We had some old morphine capsules in the First Aid locker, so I reasoned, *He's in pain, I'll give him some morphine. But how? How much? Where does it go? It's his thumb, so, if it's going to work, the best and nearest place would be his forearm.* I spent some time trying to get the needle in, squeezing the capsule, which was made of soft metal. (I have since learnt it was called a 'syrette', as was used in World War Two, and was similar to a superglue tube today.)

The boat arrived, and we were on our way to the nearest landing to the hospital. All of a sudden I remembered that I hadn't squeezed the morphine to the end of the needle – hence the problem I'd had in getting the morphine in. Any moment now the bubble of air would cause a blockage and the bosun would die! The taxi was waiting. A short drive to the private hospital where I knocked on the door and a rather large, stern nurse arrived to receive the patient. I quickly explained that I'd given him a morphine injection, even filling in a card with date and time. She took one look at him, one at me, ushered him in and closed the door in my face. *Phew, that was a close shave*, I thought, as I returned to the ship. Actually, except for the 'air thing', according to Wikipedia I did all right. Apparently, a syrette is described in the film *Saving Private Ryan*.

Looking back, I can't help feeling surprised as I remember just how many quite serious accidents had occurred on the *Ettrickbank* during my time as ship's doctor.

White crews are known to be pretty tough. On another occasion, a crew member in Auckland presented me with a penicillin syringe from the doctor. He showed me where the nurse had injected him in the arm, so I thought, *Might as well use the same hole*, and duly stuck the needle in. He didn't die, and came back for more the next day.

Seamen had cholera injections every six months, then smallpox, typhoid and typhus. After a period of time, we accumulated record booklets of when, what, and where these had taken place. In 1954, the *Sheilbank* (my first ship), had docked in Calcutta. As described earlier, the heat and long hours were exhausting, but it wasn't long after successfully tying up that we were all summoned on deck. The word got round: "Get as near to the front of the queue as you can," for Doctor 'Gangooli' (true!) was about to administer my first cholera injection and, yes, he only used *one* needle. Did he change it before injecting crew member number 70? Maybe he did 35 for deck crew and 35 for engine room, but I didn't stay to watch. I can still remember my astonishment when, sometime later in Hong Kong, the medics used a fresh needle for each person. Just imagine the crew all lined up, arms bared, ready for the big skin puncture. Such was life at sea.

Chapter 9
What *not* to do at Sea!

My time at sea was not yet over, and my Christian life was becoming ever more fragile as I spent more time at sea, away from any Christian input.

We often sailed from Bangkok to a small island where we had to approach very slowly before dropping anchor, taking soundings very carefully from a launched lifeboat going ahead of the ship, and using an old-fashioned lead-line. Once we were secure, a couple of floating warehouses would come alongside, loaded with timber, then we would up the anchor and away down the Malay Peninsular coast via Singapore again, and up to Rangoon – then the capital of Burma – where, a few miles up the Rangoon river, we loaded more hardwood logs; these were so heavy they were virtually submerged and heavily chained. I remember seeing a young lad fishing off the log raft. He had tied a chain on to his line, as a weight, and I just thought it would go straight to the bottom, but the ebb tide was so fierce that the chain lay out almost horizontally, just dipping below the river surface, such was the speed of the river. Another striking feature of those waters was the giant manta rays leaping high into the air, before crashing down, creating huge splashes in the sea. Not a place to fall overboard!

By the end of our stay in Rangoon we were fully loaded. Slipping our moorings at slack water, the pilot safely negotiated the *Ettrickbank* into the vast delta of the Irrawaddy, and once again we were en route to Ceylon (Colombo) for bunkers, tea, desiccated coconut, mail and then south-west to Mauritius. In those days, Mauritius was French speaking, but British, whereas the small island of Reunion, which lay to the south-west, was French.

Mauritius was a strange stopping place. All we loaded was a few hundred tons of very strong rum for South Africa but, being highly inflammable, this had to be stowed in a very accessible spot, ready to be swiftly dumped over the side in case of fire. As a crew we never went ashore there, but found ourselves in port for two or three days, as it was Christmas 1956. I look back and wonder how it is we didn't suffer grave injury, or even die, given the following events…

Christmas Day started well enough, but with a lot of drinking. Still, I was okay, – that is, before the apprentices spiked my drink. I was aware of this, but far enough gone not to bother, although it was beginning to get a bit out of hand. (I must stress that this took place *before* my 'signpost' experience.) Anyway, we went on deck and, looking over the side, saw, painted on our ship in bold three to four foot high letters, NEWCASTLE FOR THE CUP**.** There was a Union Castle ship – a very prestigious passenger-cum-cargo ship, on buoys, a few cables ahead of us, and that did it! We managed to launch one of the lifeboats (afterwards considered a miracle, as their engines rarely worked) and about six of us fell into the boat, armed with containers full of caustic soda, usually used for cleaning, as it would strip off anything, and off we went. Of course, everyone could hear this drunken rabble shouting and cursing the Union ship.

How on earth did we survive the onslaught, as large chunks of dunnage wood were rained down on us by the other crew? But we did, and also managed to daub some caustic soda on their ship's hull. In the midst of all this, one of our guys fell into the harbour – alive with sharks – but somehow we all returned safely, and staggered to our bunks before passing out.

The next morning things got a bit serious, but extremely funny. Our third engineer, a South African, had a 22 bore air rifle, and stood there on deck, taking pot shots at the Castle ship's crew going ashore. One second they were all up and visible, and the next all down below the gunwale, with the boat going round in circles. Their chief officer came aboard for 'friendly drinks', expressing alarm that his crew wouldn't turn to, as they had been shot at! "How on earth could that be?" We expressed concern and alarm, promised to pay a return visit, and Christmas 1956 became one of those crazy events which outraged the top brass of Union Castle, but for us was a lot of fun. Needless to say, our crew had to repaint the ship's side and, by the way, Newcastle did win!

Sadly, to cap it all, our master, who regularly hit the bottle, really insulted the captain of the Union Castle ship and his wife, as well as the shipping agents and the governor of the island. He was invited ashore to a 'big do', disdained the magnificent launch with fully dressed crew that the governor sent for him, choosing instead to go in our own quite inferior boat, then surpassed himself by dancing with the captain's wife and insulting her. This fine seaman was discharged when we reached Durban, never to return as captain. We liked him, but not his dog, who tried to bite anyone who tried to approach. I have a small scar on my nose to prove it. Strangely, whenever the Old Man went ashore, the dog would change and become completely docile.

Once again, we made our way south towards Cape Town, discharged our cargo, and began the journey north again, but not before a new master (Captain Lynch) and his wife came aboard. I really liked him but, along with many seamen in those days, wasn't keen on having a woman on board, as they were generally considered unlucky. Our journey northward for Japan followed the usual pattern, a number of East African ports to Mombasa, a major seaport, and the terminus for a major rail system from inland Africa. Our cargo was completed, and our journey across the Indian Ocean began.

It was the season of the south-west monsoon, which sweeps across the sea with anything from force 3 to force 7 winds, heavy cloud and rain, all of which makes navigation by sun and stars difficult, so I was somewhat surprised when Captain Lynch asked me what I thought about building a swimming pool for his wife on the top of No. 3 hatch. Well, no problems with stability, as the *Ettrickbank* was fully loaded, but the weather would become steadily worse as the monsoon gathered pace, dumping huge amounts of rain over the Indian subcontinent. I gave my advice – "Not advisable" – but I guess the first mate agreed with the captain, and of course the captain's wife thought it was a great idea!

The pool was constructed out of spare hatch boards held together with wire rope, and kept tight with bottle screws, bolted to the deck; a couple of tarpaulins made it watertight, and then it was filled with seawater.

Every morning, it was the custom for the first mate to instruct the deck crew bosun as to work to be carried out on deck, and this included checking the fastenings of the pool. Unfortunately, things went very wrong. With the significant swell of the monsoon, the pool water was rushing from one side to the other, causing one of the bottle screws to work loose. One of the crew tried to tighten it, but managed to turn the screw the wrong way. Unlike some ships with bulwarks, the *Ettrickbank* had a flush deck, with only a rail to stop crew falling over the side. The first mate up on the bridge saw what was happening and sent an apprentice down to sort it out. Before he could do so, the corner of the pool collapsed, and the first mate, thinking the apprentice to be either trapped in between the swimming pool hatch board and the rail or washed overboard, rushed to his aid. Well, he was trapped, and had to be paid off with a nasty leg wound, but at that point, the worst happened as, with another heavy roll, half the pool collapsed, shipping tons of water over the side and with it the first mate!

It took quite a time to launch the lifeboat, as this required more steam, but the boat was launched, the engine started (amazingly), and the third mate began many 'sweeps' across the ocean. It's not always widely appreciated that seeing a person without a lifejacket in a rough sea is almost impossible, but the ship turned round and came back on reverse course to the place where the mate was thought to have gone over. Then, miraculously, the lifeboat almost ran over the mate, and we were able to get him back on board. He was in the water for a couple of hours, and later said he had just about given up, and that large fish had come near and nudged him. It took a few days for him to recover. Fortunately, the sea wasn't too cold, and he was rather large (good buoyancy!).

I'm pretty sure the captain didn't consider building any more swimming pools and – what was that about women on ships?

Trading in the Far East is nearly always exciting but very tiring. As already mentioned, all ports work 24/7, and coming in from seaward gave very little time to catch up on sleep. Still, my two years were almost up. The *Ettrickbank* had returned to South Africa and made her way up the East African coast again. Having completed her discharge of cargo from South and East Africa, we now set a course south, to load mostly timber via Iloilo, Sandaken, Bangkok, Rangoon, plus a few days in Singapore.

The climate in this part of the world is very humid. After leaving Japan, the ship owners and agents would be assessing remaining cargo space. My job as second mate was to draw up detailed cargo plans for the five holds. The cubic capacity was calculated for all cargo, whether it be hardwood logs or a box of Japanese cameras. These plans were sent off to shipping agents. On leaving the Far East, the plans would be sent to the agents in South Africa, who would then know exactly how many tons of cargo were to be offloaded, where it was, how many gangs and what transport would be required. Obviously, how to load and in what order is part of the skill of trading by sea with cargo ships, and was a major part of a deck officer's job. This determined how deeply laden a ship could be for safe passage; trading in various ports and cargo discharge. Too much for'ard results in the ship being down by the head.

The density of the sea changes from ocean to ocean, hence the strict attention given to Plimsoll marks. And what about the use of bunker fuel and fresh water? How does this affect the stability of the ship? It's not surprising therefore that ship construction and stability were a crucial part of all Ministry of Transport examinations. Of course, the same skills are required today when it comes to packing containers.

I can't remember what we loaded in Singapore – some exotic Asian goods maybe? I do know we spent enough time there for me to make a trip to the doctor's. I had developed what turned out to be a cyst below my right ear. "Do you want me to take it out?"

"Well yes, why not. At least it'll give me a bit more time ashore." Because the cyst was near my ear, I could hear the squeak of the knife as it did its job. The doctor assured me that because it was on my neck he would make the stitches small and neat. I didn't want it to spoil my chances with the girls!

Operation completed, it was back to the ship in a taxi and report to the master that his second mate had survived, as in a few hours we would be on our way again. Onward through the Straits of Malacca, Malaysia to starboard, Sumatra to port, leave the Straits and make our way through the Andaman Sea to Rangoon, just a few more logs and we were fully loaded except for the usual Mauritius rum.

As luck would have it we left on my watch. No sympathy at sea – if you can stand you are fit to stand your watch! But the *Ettrickbank* was a rusty 1937 tramp, navigation aids nil or mostly not working. All ships check bearings of lights, headlands and buoys by using the azimuth mirror fitted over the compass on the monkey island (high up), so – leave the wheelhouse, climb the ladder to the compass, bend down to sight the light bearing from the compass and, having corrected for magnetic variation and the deviation of the compass, go back down to the chartroom to transfer the readings to the chart. It was too soon for my wound, and it wasn't long before the ligatures came adrift and my neck began to pump blood.

So I panicked. I knew this lot could put on a bandage, but if the stitches burst completely how would they stop me from bleeding to death? The first mate applied cold compresses to my neck, but it was a long night of fear and thoughts about what could happen.

The next morning a decision had been made to pay me off. The apprentices were instructed to stow all my kit in my two sea trunks, and by this time the ship was putting in at Port Swettenham, a few miles up the Malaysian coast. In 1963 this was renamed Port Klang which became a container port in 1972 and is now the twelfth largest in the world, but in 1954 it was very small and surrounded by jungle. However, the ship berthed. *Thank you, God, I'm going home.* But no – a change of plan. A Mercedes saloon awaited me on the dockside and yours truly was whisked away into a jungle hospital. Once again I was totally in the hands of God. Where was this hospital? Was it hygienic? Did they know what to do? As far as I was concerned the neck was a bit of a sensitive area.

We arrived. The place appeared to be deserted. However, I recognised an operating theatre and was invited by a native doctor (well I hoped he was a doctor!) to, "Jump up on the table." By this time the bleeding had congealed to present a large swelling. "The problem is the stitches – they are too small." Out came the knife and within minutes a large lump of congealed blood was thrust in my face, looking for all the world like a large lump of liver. This was unceremoniously dumped into a bin and *large* stitches swiftly inserted, closing the wound. Back into the Mercedes and the ship, up the gangway, let go for'ard, let go aft and the *Ettrickbank* headed once more into the Straits – no going home for me. It would be at least another nine months before I would fly home.

I was given a couple of days of 'light duties' which meant simply that one of the apprentices took the azimuth bearings.

"Can you stand?"

"Yes."

"Then stand."

Two further round trips were required before I could legally leave the ship, completing this two-year contract at sea with Bank Line. I was to pay off in Singapore. Eventually Singapore hove into sight and yours truly was ready, with trunks packed and a taxi to the shipping office to sign off, then a taxi to the airport to board a four-engine piston Super Constellation back to Heathrow via Karachi and Dusseldorf. The flight took thirty hours but thirty hours of sleep was an absolute luxury. I've no idea why we stopped in Dusseldorf, but we did, and I decided to get off and wander around the airport. I had taken my sextant on to the plane as hand baggage for safe keeping, as it was valuable and an essential piece of equipment for my work at sea, so it went with me to view the shops in a German airport. After a while the loudspeaker crackled, informing passengers of another flight to the UK. A young mother and child obviously needed a hand to get to the boarding point so, without thinking, I put my sextant down to help them and did the cheerio stuff just as my flight was announced, and off I went. London was only a couple of hours away.

About half an hour into the flight I realised I'd left my sextant behind and, although the aircrew kindly allowed me to talk to the pilot who radioed Dusseldorf airport and a search was made, my sextant had gone.

I had left Ostende in January 1958 on the *Dartbank*, transferred to the *Ettrickbank* six months later in Cape Town, and paid off in Singapore on 10th December 1959 – almost two years to the day.

Home for Christmas!

Chapter 10

Time to Think

(And a Flashy Riley Sports Car!)

It was so cold after the 30 degrees in Singapore. I had now completed six years with Bank Line and had enough sea time to sit for my first mate's ticket, but I knew things had to change. My spiritual life was in tatters; physically and mentally I was low, and although I received a bit of a hero's welcome in places like my home church in Muswell Hill, once again, my former friends were no longer around. I had also lost Sheila – in fact I didn't even know where she lived any more.

Dear Mum didn't have a clue about the state I was in. Dad probably suspected it as he had spent the war years in the RAF, but if he did he never let on. Even now, thinking of him at times, trying to work out who he really was, brings up a lot of sadness: I would love to have known my dad. He worked so hard for us, Mum, my sister Liz and me, but I had to bury all that stuff. I pretended to be okay spiritually to please my mum, although she hated me smoking. In fact it was Mum's constant nagging that triggered the process of stopping. I went to church and again pretended, behaving in a kind of gung-ho way – after all, I'd been travelling round the world for six years – but I desperately needed some friends. I must have endured the winter with some difficulty after years in the tropics, but at least Mum's good cooking ensured I put on some weight.

My studies now obliged me to travel into the City of London to Sir John Cass College. These studies took three months. I was relatively well off financially for my age (twenty-two). Some quirk in the government's ruling allowed the shipping company to pay us less whilst on study leave, so every week I, with others studying alongside me, dashed down Whitechapel Road to the dole office to collect our permitted benefit payments – always embarrassing, as so many who were there were really struggling in life, whereas we were well-dressed, loud, cocky and treated it all as a joke.

I enjoyed the studying, bought an amazing Riley sports car – bright red, very flashy, very brash. The girls loved it! Sadly, it never ran well – overall a big waste of money. I so wanted to belong. The college was linked with Holloway College in Egham, Surrey and we went there for dances, though I always landed up alone. However, despite all the ups and downs, my outward facade was that of a successful Merchant Navy officer, with not a care in the world.

My circumstances had to change. If I went back to Bank Line I'd be a first officer within a year or two, but was that going to mean another two years away? Thoughts of Sheila returned, but any attempt on my part to discover her whereabouts failed. A change of shipping company seemed to be the best option.

I was drawn to Shaw Savill so joined them – a better class of company that ran passenger as well as cargo ships to Australia and New Zealand. They owned *Dominion Monarch*, a troop carrier in the war, *Southern Cross*, one of the first passenger ships to have engines aft, and also the four 'ics' – first class passenger ships, the most famous being the *Gothic*, which was to become Queen Elizabeth II's royal yacht for her voyage to Australia, after her coronation. Shaw Savill was originally tied in with the White Star Line (of Titanic repute, another 'ic'). The ships were fast in comparison with Bank Line tramps: out through Suez, then home – a great circle track across the Pacific to the Panama Canal and home, in four to six months.

The standard of the ships themselves, but most of all the standard of the officers and crews, was a lifesaver for me. I had to wear uniform all the time, had good food and my social life took a turn for the better, but unfortunately I had to start back as fourth officer, whereas in Bank Line I had been third mate at the age of nineteen.

My first Shaw Savill ship was the *Ionic*. I joined her in Liverpool in October 1960, paid off in February 1961 in Victoria docks, London, re-joined after two weeks' leave, leaving for Australia and New Zealand, to return 28th June the same year. Two round trips in just eight months! The great thing was I was getting into the Southern Ocean for the southern hemisphere's summer and returning to the UK for our summer. It was well-known that white crews (all Shaw Savill crews were white) filled in time by selling deckchairs on the beaches, or cleaning windows in the UK summer, returning to sea when it started to get cold. Because of the short trips my time at home now became considerably less, but the time 'down under' so much more.

The *Ionic* sailed out of Liverpool with a general cargo – anything you could think of: magazines (*Women's Own* for Christmas), toilets, furniture, (on one trip we took 100 tons of fishheads for swordfishing in the Bay of Islands, NZ), cars, agricultural machinery, cloth, carpets, quantities of iodine salt, people's personal effects, whisky in barrels (especially from Glasgow), toys for Australian and New Zealand shops, clothing, shoes and anything else that could be bought in UK shops. All these were in crates and neatly stowed by hand. Occasionally we also took people's pets which were secured on deck in kennels, and on one occasion a prize ram from South Africa to Buenos Aires.

I spent five years with Shaw Savill, sat my master's ticket in 1963 and was now, officially, on paper, a master mariner in just under ten years since signing my indentures as an apprentice. However, although considered ready for promotion to chief officer, I only gained the position of second mate with this company, as I had not been with them long enough to be grounded in the company's ways and vacancies for the position were scarce as not enough masters were retiring. Meanwhile, circumstances were changing and I was becoming increasingly aware of the call of God on my life, despite the wounds and trauma.

I found wonderful fellowship and friendships 'down under'. The Aussies and Kiwis refused to work after 2100, and no weekends except Saturday mornings. As frozen carcasses were loaded and stowed by hand, if it rained, all work stopped. It wasn't uncommon to stay eighty days on the coast, discharging and loading. A strike or two helped, and I just fell in love all over again with Australia and New Zealand.

I had always loved navigation and on the *Ettrickbank* (Bank Line), under Captain Williams, it had been all about coastlines and how much current you could pick up to save time by navigating close to the African Coast and other such skills, gained through experience. However, I gradually began to lose my love for navigation; I had no love of the old magnetic compasses which required adjustment on a regular and frequent basis, depending on the course steered.

Imagine my delight, therefore, when I found that Shaw Savill ships had gyro compasses; these were much easier to use. Incidentally, for our exams we were required to strip these down and know the physics required for the compasses to run accurately. A gyro was accurate to +1 or -1 degree, therefore always pointing north +1 or – 1.

Shaw Savill ships turned their radars on 50 miles plus from the coast. It all seemed automatic. What was the point now of looking at the chart, assessing the mountains, hills, heights and lows? In Bank Line I used to enjoy drawing pictures on the charts: land 10 miles, bearing 250 degrees, weather fair, visibility good; tide running to east setting us down towards dangerous rocks. Well, it's true I enjoyed all that, but I had to get used to the changes. The master was happy and it could be argued that the ship was safer.

Meeting up with new friends in Australia and New Zealand was great, but meeting with old ones equally exciting, including Andrew and John Biggs in Melbourne and the Whitecrosses in Auckland. The Biggs' father was a Baptist minister, the Whitecrosses were Brethren and had three lovely daughters: Connie and her husband were missionaries in Japan; Ruth said she hated me and was a fiery redhead; Janet and I liked each other, but seamen have a habit of sailing off and months later she was married and looking to serve the Lord with her husband in Papua New Guinea.

I used to love going to Lyttleton in the Banks Peninsula, South Island, New Zealand, a small port, tucked into one of the inlets very much like Norwegian fiords. 'Aussie' Rickson was an Australian who lived in New Zealand with his Norwegian wife, just above the port. By the time I met him he was retired, a stocky, powerful man with light blue eyes that blazed when he told a story, and fists very often clenched when he made a point. He was an ex-sailing ship sailor who seemed to be known in whatever port one visited. His witness to Jesus was fearsome and his testimony dramatic: his ship had been in Sydney and Aussie was ashore with some of his crewmates. After a few drinks they found themselves in one of Sydney's parks where a large crowd had gathered around an open-air preacher proclaiming the gospel. Aussie became threatening, fists bunched, ready to lay out a drunk staggering around the edge of the crowd: "If he comes near me I'll deck him!" Well the drunk did, but before Aussie could land one on him, the drunk mouthed the words, "Are you saved?" All of Aussie's life flashed before him and there and then he gave his life to Jesus. He never looked back, his Christian life bold and strong, but also with love.

It didn't take long to cross the Indian Ocean and begin our discharge in Australia – usually Adelaide, Melbourne, Sydney, Brisbane and sometimes Cairns and Rockhampton, then across the Tasman Sea to New Zealand to complete our discharge in Auckland, Wellington, Christchurch and other smaller ports like Lyttleton, Timaru and Port Chalmers.

Except for the passenger ones, Shaw Savill ships were refrigerated. Modern ones like *Ionic* were 'air-cooled', just like our modern fridges. Older ships had brine pipes covering the inside of the ship holds. It was not unknown for pipes to crack in bad weather because of the hogging, sagging and panting (movements) of the ship, hence a reduction of speed was necessary in bad weather. The cargo ships carried general cargo from the UK to Australia and New Zealand, returning with thousands of tons of frozen meat, butter, wool dumps and everything else from sheep, such as bonemeal, dried blood and offal for dog and cat food. Railway trucks came alongside and slings of frozen lamb were loaded into the hold and stowed individually, by hand, so many hundreds of tons for Hull, so many for London, so many for Liverpool. Every part of the sheep was used and shipped to the UK. Our joining of the Common Market put a total stop to this trade with the UK, and overnight Australian and New Zealand farmers and traders lost their livelihoods.

On one memorable occasion on an outward voyage to New Zealand, we had loaded a number of cardboard boxes full of millinery buckram hat shapes. These were very popular with New Zealand ladies going to millinery classes. Having steamed through the Suez Canal, we were required to call in at Djibouti for oil bunkers before crossing the Indian Ocean to Australia and New Zealand. The natives here were tall, fine-looking Africans with lots of hair 'coiffed' with what appeared to be dried mud, punk style. It wasn't long after the hatches were opened, in order to load a few tons of beans, that we heard screams of laughter breaking out; the Africans had broken into the cartons of hats, stuck them on their high-rise hairdos and were running around the ship, screaming with laughter. Of course, we too were almost helpless with laughter, but the hats had to be returned, even if damaged, and watchmen placed in the hold until the cargo was complete and we were ready to leave. Fortunately all cargo is insured. I wonder how the insurance claim was worded: 'X number of hats taken after cargo workers broke into the cartons'?

We returned to the UK via Suez, calling in at a number of Mediterranean ports, carrying out a quick discharge, as the owners wanted us back home in Victoria Dock, London as soon as possible.

After a few days at home I joined another ship – the *Afric*, heading first for New Zealand then returning with some of the cargo destined for Liverpool. Weather was always a possible problem in that area. Severe gales in the Irish Sea meant the *Afric*, on which I now served, should really have delayed from leaving Liverpool, but the decision to leave was made. I was third mate and called up to the 'Old Man's' cabin for a briefing. The tug had to pull us out into the Mersey River, with the wind and tide pushing us in the opposite direction. The master and pilot were concerned that the tug cable might break; if it did, anyone caught by it would be cut in half. My station for leaving and arriving at any port was the fo'c'stle head, and the fo'c'stle crew were told to take cover. Any sign of the tow rope breaking and I was to order the tug master to let go and feed it down the ship's side, where the tug would pick it up.

Seamen use terms like 'two anchors down' and 'steaming full ahead' and over the radio several ships were doing just that in the Irish Sea that night, to prevent them from going aground. Usually the pilot disembarked off Holyhead, but not on this occasion. The rolling was so fierce that one of the air-conditioning motors was ripped off its seating on the funnel deck, landing on the boat deck below, before crashing over the side. Conditions in the Irish Sea, with wind and tide, can be as bad as anywhere in the world, except for the Southern Ocean storms which have huge rollers coming in from the Antarctic.

Once round the Lizard we made good time passing the Sovereign Light Vessel and up to the Thames Estuary where the river pilot brought us safely into Victoria Dock and home once again.

Chapter 11
Decisions! Decisions!

During my time with Shaw Savill I was once again drawn back to Jesus. Frequent home visits and the many Christian friends 'down under', particularly in New Zealand, encouraged me to read the Word, pray and seek God. On one of these times back home I went to a North London Keswick Convention where I heard a very precious elderly man, the Reverend Alan Stibbs, speak from Hebrews 6:4–6. Tough verses: 'It is impossible for those who have once been enlightened… who have fallen away, to be brought back to repentance.' These very verses, which I believe have put fear into the hearts of many 'proper' Christians, were the ones which turned the tide for me. I sat on my own, on a hard wooden chair in a half-empty tent, and made a decision: *My worldly pleasure experience has failed; my previous Christian experience has failed, but I'll give it another go*. I felt no emotion and little conviction, but the dawning of fresh hope. I knew that God forgave me there and then, but it wasn't until eight years later that I came to a place where I could finally forgive myself. I just couldn't believe I'd fallen so far away from my teenage love of the Lord.

However, meanwhile I still had to complete one more trip at sea. Deep down I was still lonely, but Father God was drawing me back to Himself. I began to further question my career. I would need to stay at sea for many years before I could become a senior officer, even though I had a master's certificate. Did I want to carry on at sea indefinitely? Seamanship was changing, becoming more automated and for me, less interesting. I was to learn that sometimes God allows us to become disenchanted with our current situation in order to move us on into the plans and purposes He has for us.

Attending Muswell Hill Baptist Church at home, from time to time, reminded me of weeks in India, meeting missionaries, hearing testimonies of young men and women who had literally forsaken everything to serve and follow Jesus. Did my Heavenly Father want me to serve Him full time? Thinking of India also reminded me of the shortage of men serving God in India. I no longer had any need to smoke or drink – the vision of the signpost in the Indian Ocean reminded me so much of the grace of God.

Then I had a big scare in Auckland. I was duty officer, responsible for the ship's safety: check the moorings, make sure cargo has been completed for the night, hatches closed, gangway safe, any parties ended and all guests ashore. The crew had had a party with lots of drink and girls and my rounds took me to their quarters. "Have a drink, Second Mate." *Help! How do I get out of this?*

I agreed to have a beer but then a crew member thrust a glass full of vodka into my hand. "Have an officer's drink!" This was a difficult situation which needed defusing. My response was to agree and down it all in one go. Shock all round and off I went to the engineers' smoke room where a more sophisticated party was in full swing. I sat down, refusing any more drink, but the burning feeling that began to take over my toes and feet was moving up my body. I just made it back to my cabin before passing out. How long I was there I don't know. That could have been the end of my sea career, but I came to, wobbled my way around to check the ship and parties, and managed to get all visitors off with the help of the ship's watchmen. So much for an officer's drink!

I don't know if there was any particular moment when I knew I had to check out my 'calling' or stay at sea. My seaman's discharge book shows a marked change in my movements around that time. The last entries bar one showed all home trade. I had gone to the Shaw Savill shipping office and spoken to the chief superintendent, told him I was a Christian and wanted to test out whether I was to stay or leave to do something else. He granted me three weeks extra leave but asked me if, in the meantime, I would be prepared to be second mate on a number of different ships, relieving officers who went on leave. It was hard, with a number of 24-hour standbys. A North Sea pilot came aboard and we spent many a night and day navigating the North Sea ports. I learnt so much. My discharge book shows eight home trade voyages and any regular port between Glasgow, Avonmouth, London, Dunkirk, Bremerhaven, Antwerp, Rotterdam and back to London.

The time came for my promised extra leave. I think I spent most of it in prayer. Again, I heard no particular voice, but became more and more convinced that I had to leave the sea. The shipping company made it very clear they didn't want me to leave, but how good it was to shake hands in good spirit with, "Well done," ringing in my ears. Another journey was before me, but this time nothing at all like the discipline, certainty of purpose and direction that, after eleven to twelve, years was ingrained in me. I was to learn that life ashore was tough, but in a very different way.

Eight years after the Keswick Convention, having met and married Helen, I was sitting in her father's church, drinking in the love and presence of Jesus, when, despite knowing that I had been forgiven, I realised I still hadn't forgiven myself. It had taken me all that time to arrive at this understanding, during which time I had completed my five years with Shaw Savill, left the sea, spent two years at Bible college in Glasgow (with a view to going to India as a missionary and funded by my sea pension) and was living in East London.

What was it that old deacon, Mr Ford, had said all those years ago? "You'll be disappointed in yourself, but don't give up." Now I understood!

I remember just saying, "Jesus, I'm so sorry; I know You've forgiven me and now I forgive myself." It certainly wasn't easy, and I still struggle from time to time with 'only His righteousness', but, as another hymn puts it:

All the way my Savior leads me
What have I to ask beside?
Can I doubt His tender mercy
Who through life has been my guide?

An incredible hymn by Fanny Crosby, with the last couple of lines:

This my song through endless ages
Jesus led me all the way.

And so it was, as John Newton had penned the words so many years before:

Amazing grace, how sweet the sound that saved a wretch like me;
I once was lost but now am found; Was blind but now I see.

PART II

LIFE ASHORE

Chapter 12
A Fish Out of Water

The whole way of life at sea was to enable a ship to travel from A to B. For an island nation like the UK the transportation of goods around the world is vital for our economy and I was a very small part of that. My training had not failed, but would it work ashore?

Prior to leaving Shaw Savill and my discussions with the superintendent, I had spent time with my home church leaders, sharing with them what I believed God was calling me to. I felt drawn to India, having sailed with lascar crews and been so wonderfully encouraged at Carey Baptist Church, Calcutta, as well as by the principals of Calcutta Bible College. To this day I remember some of the students, many of whom were disowned by their families when they became Christians, and yet totally trusted in God. The church leadership felt it right for me to 'test the call' and recommended a two year course at the Bible Training Institute, Glasgow.

I paid off my last ship in July 1964 and arrived in Glasgow in the September, to begin what turned out to be a difficult time. The fees came to the full amount of my sea pension. I had to buy study books, plus a blazer with the college badge, and a tie; I already had the grey trousers. Anyway, wearing a uniform was normal for me. What wasn't normal was three hundred students, divided more or less 50-50 male and female, in a very different world. I was truly 'a fish out of water'. The rules seemed mostly stupid to me; who had ever heard of a master mariner being told by a 'boy.' just out of public school, to turn off his room light at 11 p.m.?

Studying was difficult. I didn't even have English literature at O-Level, let alone start to try and understand Greek.

The 'Wee Man', as the principal was known, was a saintly man of God who brought the Bible to life pastorally. Other lecturers, to me, seemed… well, they weren't ships' officers, that's for sure. I was used to a spade being called a spade, not all this lovey-dovey stuff!

And, as for the 150 women, they hardly looked attractive in their dull grey uniform skirts, white blouses and blue jumpers. Some I liked and got into trouble over, as permission had to be given before even doing the simplest thing together, such as walking down the road. The building itself was known as 'the grim grey castle', practically black on the outside from the sooty emissions from the factories of Glasgow's industrial past.

This book is not intended as a record of BTI, but I learnt so much. Twice a week a fellow student and I would board a bus to Easterhouse, notorious for poverty and crime. For two years we knocked on doors, helped in the local church, and preached in the open air, as well as travelling to a number of different churches on Sundays to preach. Unexpectedly, I actually obtained top marks for elocution and enjoyed it so much that I wanted to continue for another year, but the elocution course was restricted to one year only.

My sea career had produced eleven to twelve years of self-preservation. I had survived, but it would be a few years before I began to learn who I really was (or at least, according to some, to be 'socialised'!). On one occasion the principal came knocking on my door. *Oh, what now?* I thought. I had once again transgressed the rules by walking down the road with a young lady, even if only to spend an afternoon reading the Bible on Glasgow Green. I protested angrily, at which this gracious man simply replied, "You have no idea of the sensitivities of the soul."

"Rubbish!" I retorted rudely. "What a lot of rubbish!" I had a lot to learn before I came to understand this, but it hurt. I was confused and lonely; I didn't understand what was required of me; and surprise, surprise, no one tried to get alongside to help me understand. Once again it felt as if I was cast adrift. Once again the survival instincts kicked in and Gale was in preservation mode.

After two years I gladly left BTI behind and returned home, thinking and praying, *Lord, what do I do now?* Thoughts and hopes of India were still with me, and because of that I was well regarded by my church – after all, they didn't know many who gave up the sea to go to India – but at the age of twenty-nine I was alone again. Again, it seemed that no one was willing or able to see the problems I was experiencing with being ashore or fitting in with church life so, once again I hid myself, took on the 'joker' persona and pretended everything was all right.

Meanwhile, I tried a few friendships with some of the young ladies I had come to know in the youth fellowship; I guess I was looking for the 'right one', but with no success. However, one mature couple, David and Ida Powell, became a second dad and mum for me and were largely responsible for me meeting my Helen, my future wife. I spent hours with them, initially to help David paint his house. I can remember taking every window out and reseating the glass, which took at least 30 pounds of putty. Ida fed me and listened! At last someone was listening and what was very significant for me, was that I discovered I was liked and even loved by someone. Yes, at sea I'd met many Christians and I guess had become a bit of a hero, as a Christian at sea for a long time and a long way from home, but in the long run it was always goodbye.

I became interested in the Bible & Medical Missionary Fellowship (BMMF), and they decided I needed 'church experience', but my pastor decided a placement in my home church, Muswell Hill Baptist, was not appropriate. "They might call you Michael." (i.e. They'd be too familiar!) The BMMF was interested in attracting young people through sailing, and that summer I spent a number of weeks sailing Bermuda rigged yachts up the east coast from Maldon, Essex, sleeping in the cockpit when the 'sailors' were girls. Helen, who came with me on one of these trips, remembers a particularly crazy Easter training week when the weather ranged from freezing fog and hail to extreme heat and, as a 'rookie' she spent much time up for'ard with her feet in the loo and her head out through the hatch, ringing a bell to alert other boats, as we took the risk of creeping along in fog to catch up with the other yachts in the flotilla.

I soon found myself in East London, where the Reverend Paul Tucker from East London Tabernacle encouraged the Reverend Tony Knowles of Victoria Park Baptist Church to give me the opportunity to work alongside him in the church. No finance was available, but I was offered a spare room in his home. I had to get a paying job for living expenses. And so began a remarkable time of experiencing God's provision, and then learning what it was like to live in East London, halfway between Victoria Park and Mile End station.

East London was dirty and poor at a time when most churches really struggled for a congregation. I felt trapped and almost unable to breathe after the air of the world's oceans. Would I help with the Lifeboys – the pre Boys' Brigade age group? I tried, but hated it. My main task for the church was to deliver a Christian newspaper to local houses, talking with people and occasionally with a few younger folk in the church. It was three months before I knocked on a door and discovered Mrs Dowley. Being invited into someone's home after so long brought tears to my eyes. Mrs D and her husband Roger were pioneers, having come from a well-to-do family, yet living in an ordinary terraced house with their three children, who attended local schools. Roger was dour and had inherited his father's legal practice in the City.

Twice a week, he and Ruth invited half a dozen young people in their twenties to eat stew and listen to his passion for the lost of Tower Hamlets. His wall map of Tower Hamlets had a number of pins indicating the homes inhabited by Christians in that area. Because of his work, he was able to buy and do up old terraced houses, known locally as 'Dowley houses', then offer the accommodation to Christians, with the aim of placing a Christian in each street – students from Imperial College, teachers, nurses from the London Hospital and others working in London. We sat, ate, argued and discussed how to get alongside indigenous East Enders, and how to lead them to Christ. I was there for seven years and before Helen and I left, the nearby East London Tabernacle, which had been more or less empty after a rebuild following wartime bomb damage, was bursting at the seams. Nearly all had been invited into Dowley homes and found Jesus as Saviour. So great was the impact of Ruth and Roger that the council named two streets after them after they moved to Bermondsey.

With the help of a lovely Christian Cypriot lass in the job centre, I found a job to pay the bills, writing commercial vehicle licences for the Ministry of Transport in Soho Square, mornings only, but oh boy, was that a blow to my pride. I even had to take a test because of my lack of GCE O-level qualifications (with questions like 'What's the third month of the year?'), even though the same MOT office had awarded me a master's ticket in 1963! It was so hard sitting there, with sealed windows, cigarette smoke and a master's certificate that could get me a job anywhere in the world at the drop of a hat, burning a hole in my back pocket. But God had me there for a reason.

My greatest love in East London developed out on the streets, where I started talking to teenagers. Would they like a club? I got a lot of stick, but with the church's blessing we could use the church hall on Friday nights. The local council gave us a lot of equipment, as well as a full set of football kit, and we joined one of the East London football leagues, as well as playing in the floodlit league. Hackney Marshes had at least 150 pitches and, over time, our team improved. I obtained some good players and sat my referee's certificate. The club grew to about 60 members but, most of all, I got to know a group of a dozen lads, plus a few of their girlfriends, really well. In time, some of this group became like family and would arrive at the flat early morning, change into work gear, go to work, come home, change again and go out with the 'birds', often bringing fish and chips back late evening. We spent most evenings in my flat, sometimes into the early hours. Yes, by this time I had a flat *and* some money to pay for it.

Friday nights usually became a bit of a problem. About two in the morning a knock on the door and two or three of the lads would stagger in, the worst for drink, sometimes drugs. What to do? Call the police or call a doctor?

Decision made, they'd spend the night on the floor under a blanket, eventually coming round, then off to the famous Roman Road market.

By now ideas of India as a mission field were fading.

Then another story of God's grace. Through the club I started to visit local schools, talking to headteachers about involving the young people in community work. A visit to South Hackney Comprehensive School resulted in a conversation with the head of maths; would I like to teach CSE maths to the fourth and fifth years? Me a teacher? Never! I hated teachers! But I was persuaded; the maths and physics used in my sea career were considered adequate and so, almost overnight, my £6.10 shillings from the MOT became over £20 a week – hence the flat.

I was asked to attend County Hall for an interview. *Well, that will be the end of that*, I thought. A tall, bronzed gentleman addressed me in a very grand and intimidating room. He hadn't read my application papers, but quickly scanned them, before looking up and exclaiming, "But you haven't any qualifications! What are you doing?" I explained that I was a Christian and trying to help the young people in Tower Hamlets. He looked hard at me for a moment, then stuck out his hand, said, "Congratulations on your new job," and I was dismissed. The head of the school had to reassure me that I was indeed now on his staff as an unqualified maths teacher.

Whilst all this was going on, God was preparing a wife for me, to share the journey ahead. It was after five years in East London that I met Helen. The lads were in awe. They had initially viewed me with suspicion: thirty-two and not married? But I had been telling them that God would give me a wife. To her embarrassment, from the very first meeting, Helen became known as 'Mrs Mick', and seven months later, on 29 March 1969, four of the lads came to our wedding. I would no longer walk alone. (It seems our first date held even more embarrassment for Helen, as we called in at my parents' home and and I apparently introduced her to my mother with the words, "Hi, Mum, meet the wife!")

During this time we also became involved with a new church plant, where Helen played a little portable organ at the consecration of a terraced house in Hackney, led by Bishop Trevor Huddleston, newly back from South Africa's apartheid struggles.

I was now living in a mission field and secretary of the Eastern Region of Frontier Youth Trust (part of Scripture Union). By this time I believed teaching was right for me, so went to Whitelands College (Roehampton Institute) for three years, qualifying for a B.Ed (Bachelor of Education degree) as well as obtaining a distinction in Youth and Community Studies.

A plum job came up as tutor-warden in London's Inner London Education Authority at St Paul's Way School, just off the Mile End Road. This meant I taught a 25% timetable and also ran a large youth and community wing in the school, after hours, with annual enrolments of over a thousand, and thirty part time staff members. This was yet another story of God's love, grace and leading, but by now we had a young son, Richard, born in the Salvation Army's Mother and Baby

Hospital, Hackney and, with surrounding demolition works leading to dead mice in the oven and mould in the cellar and on the shutters of the windows of our little flat, we were forced to look further afield for healthier living accommodation.

One evening, my art class tutor said, "Why don't you look around Strood, it's only thirty to forty minutes' drive away from the school." With family help we bought a modern three-bedroom house in Cuxton, just outside Rochester, and with this, another chapter of our lives began to unfold. We were sad to leave East London, as we loved the people there, but the lads we'd spent so much time with were growing up anyway, getting married and moving away. Sadly, to my knowledge, not one of them accepted Jesus into their lives, but one did come to me, saying he really did understand what sin, hell and salvation were, but was not yet prepared to give his life to Jesus. I wonder if he did? Seven years, Lord? 'One sows and another reaps.'! (John 4:37) We still remember them with great affection and prayer.

Chapter 13
Transition

CUXTON – Described as 'a Kentish Village'. From the house the River Medway could be seen, and running parallel with the river was the railway into Strood and Rochester and the A228 which connected easily with the A2 and London. We'd never lived in the country before. Our house was a modern semi with a lounge/diner where Richard could now charge up and down. At long last I could breathe fresh air and see vistas of the North Downs, as well as try to jog over them.

Once again Father was opening up another opportunity to serve Him. (Remember my baptismal hymn: *O Jesus I have promised to serve Thee to the end. J.E.Bode)*

I continued working at St Paul's Way school Community Centre for another two years, before pressure of travelling and late hours became the main factors in my quest for a more local job, and I was offered and accepted a post as Head of Careers and Social Studies in Northfleet, Kent. The career aspect was very interesting, visiting many of the industries located on the Thames, but the biggest event at that time was the birth of our daughter, Nicola Rachel, in the front room. So now we were four. Helen soon found friendships with other mums, which tied in well with our church life.

Cuxton had an Anglican church at the top of the hill and a small United Reformed (URC) chapel at the bottom, which was affiliated to a much bigger church in Rochester (The Vines). The corrugated iron chapel was painted green on the outside and varnished brown inside and was 'home' to one other couple with three sons and a few 'attenders' to begin with. Helen was often heard to say that we needed an 'Act of God' to demolish this 'tin hut' so that it could be replaced with something better so, when one morning a neighbour called to say that it was on fire, the general consensus was, "Helen did it!" Until a new, brick-built annex could be built we worshipped together in homes, which brought about a new dimension of intimacy in our worship and fellowship.

At this time the charismatic Fountain Trust Movement was influencing the Medway towns in a big way: The Vines had come alive evangelistically and with the Holy Spirit. After six months and following the sudden death of the member who was holding everything together, I was asked if I would take over as chapel superintendent and also be an elder of the main church. Helen and I agreed, with the understanding that we wouldn't be obliged to carry out or teach anything contrary to our understanding of Scripture, for example child baptism. This issue never arose, but we used to borrow the baptistry at Borstal Baptist Church in the next village, where with the senior minister, Stan, I had the joy of carrying out a number of believers' baptisms. We still laugh at the memory of the time when Stan and I entered the church from the vestry, dressed in our protective clothing – Stan in custom-made waterproof gown, complete with epaulettes, and me in borrowed salmon fishing dungaree waders! As I went to sit down at the end of the opening hymn, the stiff waterproof outfit resisted, and I was shocked into blurting out, "But I can't sit down!" as I realised I couldn't bend, and collapsed onto a hastily provided stool, amidst gales of laughter.

The fellowship numbers grew and many precious friendships were made. Blessing certainly flowed. A fiery Canadian visiting preacher – a friend of Helen's family – scared the life out of me in my first encounter with the deliverance ministry, which certainly brought a different dimension to our spiritual understanding. One significant family, George and Phyl Speirs with their three children, Ian, Nigel and Hilary, became committed members of the chapel and were a huge encouragement to us as a family. They also became much-loved 'holiday mum and dad' to our two tots. We are still in touch with the family. Only a few years ago I met up with Ian and his wife at his father's funeral. Ian has an amazing story of the healing and grace of God. His mother was told he would always be a cabbage, as he suffered from severe epilepsy, and we spent many an hour helping and praying for him as a young adult, particularly when he had as many as eleven consecutive seizures. Little did I know that when on one Sunday I threw out the rhetorical question, "I wonder if anyone here will hear the call to be a missionary abroad," Ian did. His story is written elsewhere, but he spent years in Portugal, pioneering services for the disabled, having married a disabled Brazilian woman. They also worked with WEC (World Evangelisation Crusade), touring with the Joni Eareckson film *Joni* and escorting many groups of UK young people abroad, to enthuse young Christians and encourage embryonic fellowships.

Our time in Cuxton was precious. Yes, we had many battles, but also much fun, and God blessed a number of lives; some have sadly turned away, but others have continued with the Lord, and it's amazing to know we have had some input into their lives, as they have into ours. It's really humbling to hear how God has called out others, generations being blessed and, in turn, taking up leadership challenges.

A few years ago, a surprise phone call informed us that the chapel was now in Kent's Open Air Life Museum, near Maidstone, as an example of a building that was still fulfilling the function for which it was built over a hundred years previously.

Helen and I visited and, with great delight, learnt it was still being used as a venue for the Alpha Course 'Away Day' by local churches. I guess I must be one of the few pastors whose former church is now in a museum.

Chapter 14
Cambridge

Northfleet School turned out to be quite difficult and I was wanting to experience a youth and community centre that was 100% Christian. We didn't really want to leave Cuxton, where Helen was really being used by God to reach out to a number of other young mums, but news of a proposed venture in Cambridge, sponsored by five churches, attracted our attention. The group of churches included three Anglican, one Baptist and one Methodist. The latter's scarcely used buildings became the new centre, after being dramatically redeveloped. At this point we would like to say how much we have valued working with a variety of different churches over the years as we have learnt that each one has had something new to teach us and to contribute to the work of the Kingdom of God. To the above list we would add the United Reform and Pentecostal Churches.

And so it was that I answered an advert for someone to initiate and lead a new project in Romsey Town, Cambridge. At first we thought it was in lovely Hampshire, not the tatty bit of Cambridge, far removed from the grandeur of university life, but this proved to be our next step, and yet again God stepped in to make it possible.

We were accepted, but now had another problem: where to live? The money used to buy our house in Kent had been lent to us in Swiss francs by a relative who now required repayment. Changes in world finances meant we now had to repay three times the amount borrowed, so selling the house now would just cover that, leaving us with absolutely nothing to spare. Did God want us to move to Cambridge or not? Part of the answer to that question would be the provision of suitable accommodation. As the project was to be managed by the local Anglican Church, an empty curate's house, with a long garden, was offered to us and the Gale family duly moved to pioneer the new Romsey Town Churches' Youth and Community Centre, brainchild of the Reverend Peter Phenna, and commonly known as 'The Mill' –

speaking of Jesus as the Bread of Life.

We were warmly welcomed by the churches and neighbours-to-be, a number of whom offered to prepare the house for us by refreshing it with paint and paper, if we would just choose and tell them the wallpaper and paint colours we'd like. How kind! As we lay in bed that night, exhausted by the move and having settled the children in our new home, we heard strange sounds and watched as the wallpaper that had been pasted over the previous vinyl wallpaper slowly rolled down the bedroom walls. We did laugh!

Getting down to the establishment of The Mill, I saw through the completion of the building works and begged and received all the equipment needed to get the place up and running. The site was an old Methodist church in Hemingford Road and comprised a large sanctuary and a small hall. We turned the larger building into a gym-cum-games hall with a couple of flats above, and linked the two buildings, forming a coffee bar, toilets and office. My biggest headache was staffing. The supporting churches sent a couple of helpers in the form of two young people they didn't know what to do with, one an alcoholic who smoked continuously and smelled of lavender (to disguise the alcoholic clues, as we found out!) and a big Geordie who was more used to borstal institutions than polite company, but who had a big heart for wayward or downtrodden kids. The promise of 'students to help' did not materialise for some time but eventually Time for God and Care Force gap year folks did. These organisations gathered up a number of young people – usually those who had completed university or college – but we only had two at the most, so the long campaign of encouraging and then training local church folk began.

Meanwhile, it was a question of turning our hands to anything and everything; indeed, it was whilst I was swabbing out the loos one day that a visitor came looking for the warden, assuming I was the caretaker. This made us think that we should perhaps write a book one day entitled *So You Want to Serve The Lord?*, with the subtitle *Be Careful What You Ask For!* Maybe this is now that book.

God blessed the project and within a few weeks a number of clubs were launched, with some 400 people of all ages coming every week. I will never forget the first teen nights when anything up to 200 teenagers queued outside, waiting for the doors to open, with only a couple of helpers inside.

We could doubtless fill a small book recounting all the antics of the local teens: we enjoyed camping in Norfolk at an old rocket station in Swaffham and enjoyed many soccer matches – not least against the police. But for me, the highlight was our moonlight walks over the Gogs, (the only local hill in the area) when, having previously hidden kindling, sausages and frying pans, we downed our food then created mayhem on the way back, disturbing a number of courting couples in cars who thought they were well hidden!

The clubs grew rapidly: the elderly, mums and toddlers – pretty much what you would expect to find in any youth and community centre. The discos were alarming, mainly because of lack of staff, but they were also good fun. We became expert at finding illicit booze stashed in toilets and up in nearby trees for later use. A local curate converted a vehicle into what became the Romsey Town Roadshow, which took a travelling disco out into the Cambridgeshire villages. We also joined forces with a local church group for a Sunday 'film and God slot' but what worked most of all was the welcome and love shown by the congregation of a local Brethren chapel. I eventually had a number of amazing people who not only developed some remarkable youth and community skills, but also encouraged the 'Mill mob' to put on Christmas pantos, for which they wrote the script. These involved a huge amount of work, setting up the stage and bringing in all the chairs, to say nothing of cajoling moody teens into continuing rehearsals when they fell out with each other, but it was crazy, great and resulted in a production simply way beyond anything many of the 'actors' would have thought possible.

Many more stories could fill these pages but one of the most memorable was a time when half a dozen of the lads, Helen and myself, plus a helper and a young man who wanted to be a youth worker, went for a sail and canoe in one of the tributaries of the River Cam. The lads were mucking about in the water, whilst I was swimming a short distance away downstream. Suddenly loud shouts pierced the air. The young would-be youth worker had decided to try and join some of the lads on the other side of the river. The trouble was he couldn't swim and promptly disappeared under the reeds.

Those nearest to him tried to pull him out, but the mud made him too slippery and they hadn't the strength.

I got there as fast as I could, frantically wondering what on earth to do. Arriving at the spot indicated, I managed to dive down under him in the water and stood up with him on my back. Somehow, he came clear. At first, we all thought he was dead, but eventually (it seemed an age to us) he coughed out a lot of water and came round. The relief was unimaginable. Later, back at our home, I was telling the story to some of the others club members, leaving God out of the story, only to be corrected emphatically: "No, Mike, it was a *miracle*!" Yes, it truly was.

In addition to the daily work at The Mill, as secretary for the Eastern Region of Frontier Youth Trust (FYT), I travelled a lot to various village churches, as well as those in Cambridge, spreading the word that Jesus loves these kids, open your homes to them and will you come and help. We were also able to help in the training of Church of England students from Ridley Hall College, particularly those who had selected the Community Work/Pastoral Care module in their preparation for the ministry.

I must mention a very special couple, without whom we could not have managed. They were in a lot of need when they came and offered to help, but when we eventually moved on, knowing all our ups and downs, struggles, management problems and opposition, these friends said, "Mike and Helen, if God brought you to Cambridge just for us, it was right." How humbling and how worthwhile. They went on to continue serving the Lord, as they helped to lead a small Baptist church on a housing estate.

After five years of metaphorical ditch-digging and foundation building, I was exhausted; Helen had had a bit of a breakdown; Richard and Nicky were in their schools; but I yearned for a deeper experience with the Lord. However, by this time not only our bodies but also our spirits were jaded and rather negative and in no fit state to rightly discern the way forward. A timely leaders' retreat at The Hyde, Handcross, Sussex with Colin Urquart and his team restored us, and confirmed that we were in a maze and needed to find our way out. As we prayed we 'saw' the maze and a small white gate at the base of the hedging. It would mean getting down low to go through the gate, and we felt God was showing us that the way forward would require humility on our part.

It's a very long story as to how we left Cambridge. We had a growing sense that our role at The Mill was coming to an end and that it would need a fresh person to develop the project and take it forward so, over a period of about a year, we had been looking around and seeking God's will for our future. I had been reading a book by Oswald Chambers called *Not Knowing Whither,* about Abraham and the way in which he grew in faith as he and his family obeyed God.

Unbeknown to me, Helen was also being independently challenged about 'risky living' faith. There were many indicators, but the final confirmation came one day, when the five supporting churches held a joint service of thanksgiving – an important annual event in the life of The Mill. That morning I woke with severely bloodshot eyes – an optical haemorrhage, and was clearly unable to attend. Helen went without me, and on return stated bluntly and clearly, "Mike, the baby has been born." We realised we had been midwives to the project and it was now time to hand the 'baby' back to the 'parents' – i.e. the local churches and younger staff – for the next phase. (We're delighted to report that The Mill continues to thrive and develop and is still doing so today over forty years later, with an excellent reputation.)

Chapter 15
So Now What?

It was only as we were trying to explain to our daughter's schoolteacher why we were leaving Cambridge, that she commented, "You're like missionaries really, aren't you?" Well, that was a surprise, as we hadn't thought of it like that; my home church had always considered that 'missionaries go abroad'.

We tested out our 'call' with mature Christian leaders over the course of that year, and even at the last hour were willing to back down. However, it seemed right to all that we should move on. There was one possible opening in Devon and friends in Cambridge offered us the use of a garage in which to store the bulk of our belongings, plus temporary accommodation should we need to return.

And so, one sunny morning we left Cambridge in an elderly Volvo Estate, with a trailer full of stuff plus two kids, a dog and potted plants (why potted plants?); the rabbits had had to go. Our faith was high, although we still hadn't a clue what we were heading for, but it was the only open door, so through it we went. We made our way down to Devon – initially to stay with a couple in Ivybridge who, on our arrival, made it clear they didn't really want us there, expressing their concern that we might be a threat to their plans, but we were kindly offered accommodation with them for a period of two months only. It turned out that the move was to be one of the hardest things we've ever done. Sadly, we now know it was even harder for Richard and Nicki, our two children, and they found settling into their new schools and building friendships very difficult.

So, we had no home and no work. What did Abraham do? He 'built an altar to the Lord', made a number of mistakes, but continued with his walk of faith.

Helen knew a number of people in Plympton Pentecostal Church, a few miles down the road, some of whom had known her from birth, so we felt it was a good place to go – not least because Father God spoke through the gifts of the Spirit there and we so much needed to hear His voice.

We caused a bit of a stir in Ivybridge by calling in at a local estate agent asking for a house which we believed God would provide for us, but *how*? We had no money and no house to sell. Crazy? No, not if you believe His word – that when God calls, He provides. One day it actually happened – *and* within the allotted timescale. The miracle came about through Helen's family, and two months to the day we moved into our new house. This one belonged to us – or rather to the Lord.

What next? I had been doing supply teaching, which certainly kept the wolf from the door, supplemented by Helen also doing some teaching. We were attending the little church and enjoying the fellowship, though regarded by some with suspicion as to why we were there (were we a 'plant'?). The praise and worship in particular, was such a blessing. The senior pastor (a founder, along with his father and family) was having a number of blackouts, which would eventually lead to open heart surgery, and on one of these occasions I was asked to take over the service. Six months later a knock on the front door revealed one of the church elders, coming to ask if I would take over the leadership of the local church. It so happened that the very same week I was invited to apply for a permanent, full-time teaching position. The timing seemed interesting. We felt convinced that serving the Lord in this way was a fulfilment of the prayer and leading so far, so why would we simply return to teaching? So, church it was, and once again I was stepping into a completely new situation, with no real training as to how to lead a Pentecostal church family, many of whom were related and a number who didn't want me! Where had I heard that before? Who ever said the Christian life was boring!

I hardly knew where to start. Initially it was very exciting, with freedom to preach and teach and a deep sense of being in a very special place where over many years God had blessed people in extraordinary ways. The prophetic word, tongues and worship were the norm. Founder members were former methodists who had longed for a deeper walk and experience of the Lord and one of these families had had a constant stream of people arriving at their door from near and far, prompted by the Spirit and having heard of this gathering of Spirit-filled Christians.

It took me a little while before I came to realise and appreciate that this was a typically rural community. How could a world traveller and pioneering youth and community worker from urban Tower Hamlets and downtown Cambridge fit in here? The problem, and it really was a problem, was two-fold. I didn't know how to handle things and had no one really capable of helping me; the elders were godly, but totally loyal to 'the family' and the past, and probably most of all, I didn't know how damaged I was. Frustration and the 'old nature' built up and finally brought about a very sad departure. I knew I had preached quite well, encouraged a lot of prayer and sought to open horizons; neither could I forget what I had seen and experienced in India and many other places. We held an elders' meeting every Monday morning but it usually ended with the observation, "We like what you said *but…*"; my family was finding life difficult; people came and people went; my wages often depended on 'free gifts' and when at times I tried to introduce changes it didn't go down well and the air turned a religious blue!

As for dear Helen, much of my despair was taken out on her. Early in the week we would take a flask of coffee out on to beautiful Dartmoor nearby to let off steam and spend some time together. Our children were also adversely affected by the stresses and strains, though at the time we didn't realise just how much. Was there blessing? Yes, very much so, with new faces wanting to be part of God's Kingdom in today's world. I got on well with other local church leaders – in fact we turned our integral garage into a second lounge which was used for the Ivybridge Church Ministers' fraternal meetings, much to the astonishment of the new rector. He was under the impression that the house belonged to the church. "No," we said, "to the Lord."

You'll have gathered that we lived in Ivybridge, seven miles from the church in Plympton. A number of the congregation also lived here and when a new family joined us, John (not his real name) who had been a leader in several different settings, became popular. He and I formed a strong friendship and eventually it was agreed he should take over at Plympton and I would plant a new church in Ivybridge. However, not very long after handing over responsibility to John, he changed so much so quickly that I was obliged to ask him to step down for a time. This caused a huge rift between his family and me, with knock-on effects, as other church leaders in Plymouth rounded on me. It was deeply hurtful and I was blamed. I share this because of what happened later.

It wasn't long after this that a meeting I held with the church elders resulted in me finally losing my temper and walking out. After five years of leading the church, and at the age of fifty-six, I was once again looking for employment.

Eventually I found a full-time teaching post in Kingsbridge, South Hams I was very broken, but over a period of some eighteen months the atmosphere of the school, with its love and acceptance which far exceeded what I had experienced in Plympton Church, plus the care of the school staff, put me back together again. Every day I had a sense of serving the Lord in school, joyfully filling in for staff, and was amazed when two members of staff in a middle management meeting independently proposed that I should be employed as a staff 'pastor'. However, my teaching position was only temporary so, at the end of my time, I had to move on.

In the midst of all this and despite having had no contact with him for some years, due to his anger over what had transpired, out of the blue I received a phone call from 'John': "Come and see our new bungalow." It was so good to see him and his wife. It was just before Easter. We were no longer living in Ivybridge, but had moved into Plymouth and were attending a Baptist church there. John and his wife joined us there for the Easter Sunday morning service. Hugs and forgiveness all round! They couldn't come to lunch but promised to come for a meal the following Sunday. That evening a phone call from his wife brought the news: John had passed away. How glad, how blessed and how timely – John and I were reconciled. This confirmed the importance of relationships and forgiveness, and keeping short accounts – we never know if we'll have another opportunity.

Work in Plymouth schools was not easy to find, but eventually I found a post in a pupil referral unit (a unit for excluded pupils). It was tough, understaffed and with hardly any equipment, but I loved the kids. It was my last seven years of paid employment before one morning, when preparing for the day's toil, I just went blank, never to return to work, due to a breakdown and then retirement. And so ended forty-nine years of (mostly!) paid employment.

Chapter 16
Restoration

Wandering around Plymouth Hoe, it began to feel that I was back in Hornblower times: the war with France over and thousands of seamen ashore with nothing to do, no money (although in my case I had a pension), taken out of their environment and plunged into nothingness. I had always 'done stuff'. My sea career was over; youth and community work was over; teaching was over; leadership in the Lord's work was over; family grown up and living elsewhere. A phrase from a hymn described me well: 'My restless spirit finds rest in Thee' but to be honest the 'rest' bit wasn't really there. I longed for more and still do.

Sometime after my father's death, when visiting my mother, who lived in Stourbridge, West Midlands, I discovered a large family Bible in the bookcase. The front of it contained names, birth and death dates of family members, and there I came across my name and date of birth. Alongside it my dad had written 'Michael – Proverbs 7 vs 1–2'.

My Son, keep my words and store up my commands within you. Keep my commands and you will live. Guard my teaching as the apple of your eye. Bind them on your fingers. Write them on the tablet of your heart.

From my early days at Muswell Hill Baptist I had grown to love and read the Word of God and still do. Bible college had broadened my understanding. I therefore jumped at a friend's suggestion to accompany him to a conference in Brighton, run by Ellel Ministries and entitled 'Let the Oppressed go Free'. Little did I know that it was to be life-changing for me.

It was mid February 2001. The weather was good with a bright clear sky, and it was great to be out and enjoying the fresh air and light. The conference centre was the opposite – not a window to be seen in the arena where the meetings were to be held. I remember saying that it was going to be very hard for me to stay there. All my seaman's instincts were kicking in: I had to be outside in the fresh air and sunlight.

The praise and worship was good; the opening sessions were good. Already my heart was responding, and within two hours I was asking if it was possible for me to stay there. The presence of God was tangible. The theme of the conference touched on a number of people groups who had suffered slavery and oppression and already my locked up spirit was stirring. I was hearing truth with a love which, as yet in my sixty-five years, I had never heard. Or if I had, it had never registered. I began to weep, beginning to realise that Father God wanted to let the real me out. But who was this real me? That discovery would come later. The opening session was over and my friend Peter's question to me was, "Do you always cry when you come to a conference?"

"No, never."

I was to learn that over the years I had built up layer after layer of defensive protection to cover the pain and hurt, rejection and shame of failure, letting down Helen and my two children. The temper that just burst out of me when provoked often left them hurt and damaged. I was certainly not free. If not free, then I was bound, in prison, but a loving Heavenly Father had been waiting all these years to take me on the journey of restoration. For a time I cried when walking along the road; I cried in the café; I cried just about everywhere. Where was the tough seaman who had learnt to survive? Where was the pastor who so wanted to be used by God to bless others, but managed to upset a good few? My youth and community work had gone well; my teaching had gone well, especially in Kingsbridge School; and yes, I still loved the Word, but what about the rest...?

The director of Ellel Ministries, Peter Horrobin, used to say, "The church (in general) knows how to catch fish, but doesn't know how to clean them," to which I would add: "It also doesn't know how to *restore* them."

During the conference I listened to testimonies and teaching from all over the world which fitted so well with my world view, and when the invitation was given it wasn't a problem for me to go forward as an indication of my intention to move on.

Ellel were encouraging people to sign up for courses so, loaded with literature, I returned to Plymouth, knowing I had to apply for the nine-week school at Glyndley Manor, one of the full-time centres in the UK. Glyndley is near Eastbourne in East Sussex, an old manor house-cum-hotel. Its history is God's story, amazing and right at the centre of God's will and purposes.

The grand title of the nine-week school, *School of Evangelism, Healing and Deliverence 2001*, reflected the ministry of Jesus and then the Early Church – a recapturing of the full gospel in the power of the Holy Spirit. I was accepted, and the time came for me to drive from Plymouth to Glyndley. Taking our old Audi 80 enabled me to load my bike for exercise; I also joined a local gym in Hailsham, three miles from the centre. My fellow students, 33 in number, came from 17 different countries, the furthest being Australia. It took a while to shake down. Lectures were long, coffee good. I enjoyed the fellowship, especially with students whose countries I had visited.

After two weeks, a knock on the door of my room proved to be life changing. (Yes, another life-changer!) Michael Lee and Eleazar Lee, both from Singapore, asked if they could have a chat, then asked if they could come alongside me as friends and brothers for the rest of the course. This was a real gift from the Lord and very precious, as you can imagine; my years of loneliness at sea, plus years away from home had made my ability to form friendships very difficult but their insights and experience gained in leadership in Singapore opened up my understanding in a number of different areas.

A large part of the teaching centred around the healing of the soul and spirit. This was new to me, except what I had heard at the conference. There would be a time ahead when we as students would have an opportunity to share with a member of the prayer ministry team. Most of us were somewhat apprehensive, but if we were ever to be able to help others we needed sorting out ourselves. I was to learn later what a very special place that conference room was, set apart for ministry. All the staff, including the young people's housekeeping team (again from many nations) would be praying in support, even whilst going about their daily tasks. The time came for our individual appointments. Ministry team members were spaced out around the room and we were invited to go to whoever we felt would be right. It took some courage but 'that old boy over there' seemed as if he had enough experience and understanding of life to listen to me. So off I went.

"Tell me about your parents." Well, a Christian home was certainly a good place to start.

"Dad joined the RAF when I was two years old; I saw very little of him for six years."

"So your father left you, did he?"

I felt the anger rise. How dare he speak about my dad like that! After all, my dad had gone off to fight Hitler, like many other dads.

"But you were only two, you wouldn't know he hadn't abandoned you."

Within seconds he was holding me in his arms, as everything within seemed to fall apart. I wept and wept and clearly saw the root of my pain and rejection that I'd carried all my life, very successfully buried for over sixty years. Of course, I was responsible for my own actions, but within was a 'distortion' which had twisted so much of my life and helped to distort so much of my thinking, understanding and therefore behaviour.

Yes, it was tough and gut wrenching, but my Heavenly Father was meeting with me at a level I had never known. It was to take time, but the real Michael was beginning to emerge. The outwardly tough Mike put up a bit of a fight after so many years, but what was in the heart of God for me as a person was becoming a reality. Who was this Michael? I remember on another occasion shouting out in distress for all to hear: "But I don't know who I am!" Who was the real me, created in the image of God?

Glyndley and all it taught was becoming like heaven. You can imagine the depth of fellowship we as students were now able to share. I was fellowshipping at a level I'd never known before. Sitting in rows in church didn't really cut it.

Much could be said about the school: creative activity sessions played a significant part; a weekend mission with a church in Pevensey Bay; learning to do prayer ministry. Learning to pray in a different way meant waiting on the Lord for His agenda.

Nine weeks later, on a cold November day, we all had to leave. Many of us had to be almost pushed out of the front door in order for us to re-enter the world. I had made deep and real friendships with a number of students, friendships of spirit and soul. Once again, I was on the move, leaving what I had come to love, but of course, returning home after nine weeks was wonderful. Many of my fellow students had clear goals and knew where they would be going and what God was leading them into. I didn't and I found that disappointing. Where on earth was I going to fit in now? The average church was very different from what I'd been experiencing, and for some I may have seemed a bit challenging. I therefore welcomed the chance to attend the 20-day school which helped me to earth a lot of the teaching, whilst coming alongside an experienced ministry team member.

Could I learn to be an Ellel Ministries Team member? It meant travelling back and forth from Plymouth to Glyndley – a journey of approximately six hours each way, and staying for longer courses, as well as healing retreat weekends. I loved it, growing in confidence and understanding.

I loved belonging to a team, learning to listen, not only to a needy person, but also to Father God who, through the Spirit, knew exactly what a person's problem was. In many cases it was not a quick fix; very often healing was a process, but how encouraging it was when, in testimony time, delegates shared how they had met with the Lord afresh and were going home very different.

I started off as a No. 3 counsellor – each little ministry group consisted of a lead ministry team member, a No. 2 in a support role and a No. 3 trainee. I found that frustrating, but it was a good learning model. Opportunities came to take part in other courses and retreats, and soon I was very involved with Ellel. As a professional teacher I had initially decided I wouldn't apply to teach, but that changed. I loved the teaching but often found difficulty in fully understanding some areas of the ministry. My biggest problem was keeping to time, but in all fairness, we taught from notes which covered a lot of ground and therefore, with a few stories added in, time just flew by.

In 2003 I had the opportunity to go to Australia to help in a new centre at Gilbulla, just outside Sydney. I was to make up the team and Helen came as a member of the 20-day school. God had it all worked out. Helen was given three months off from work (mostly with pay), and Peter of Brighton fame, needing temporary accommodation, came to stay in our house in Plymouth, paying rent, which helped with our Australian expenses.

We decided to take advantage of the opportunity to stay on for a holiday 'down under', meeting old friends there, and then a further three weeks in New Zealand. In Sydney we met up with Mike and Ruth Broadley, mentioned because Mike and I had attended the same primary school in Finchley, North London during the war and where our mothers had been friends. Mike and Ruth lived on the edge of the Blue Mountains where bush fires threatened them every year. And so the story could go on. For me it was just like old times. During my sea career I had spent many weeks there, which often ran into months, and to be in the place I loved so much was great.

In New Zealand we had a brief opportunity to meet up with John Balchin and his wife. John had been my Old Testament lecturer in BTI Scotland. We then made a mad dash round a number of beautiful tourist places before returning home again via Singapore where things were very different because of SARS. The stopover in Singapore enabled us to meet up with Eleazar and Michael Lee (the two brothers who had befriended and supported me during the nine week school). They really spoilt us.

So many people and places were special, and returning to the rain-soaked UK was difficult, but I was learning more and more about the ministry of Ellel, taking part in a number of courses and teaching on the modular courses. However, my first love was the restoration weeks. Helen and I hosted the first few and we loved it. Helen shone, being very skilled at relationships and pastoral care. These weeks were based on Isaiah 42:22: 'But this is a people plundered and looted…' People came from different countries and situations to be part of a week which became life-changing for many.

The French week was something special; the courses were taught in English and translated into French, and prayer ministry also offered in French for a large group of people who came over from France – a country that was very dear to Helen, who had strong family links there, her mother having been brought up in Paris. We had visited her uncle, Durban Squire, and his wife, Odette, in Paris several times, and it was therefore very exciting when the opportunity arose to serve the Lord with Ellel in France, not least because Helen spoke fluent French. I didn't have any French, but somehow it didn't seem to matter, and actions often spoke louder than words – literally – and led to a great deal of fun and laughter.

Over a period of three years we spent six months in Saint-Laurent-du-Pont, not too far from Grenoble. Our role, along with others, was to help the French leaders, Patrick and Valerie Chambron, to establish Ellel France alongside their church. We learnt so much about a people who had suffered greatly through wars both religious and secular. To be fair, it would take many pages to truly describe the many ways in which God broke through into broken lives, but one in particular was amazing. We were in the church where the healing retreat was in full flow. I looked around and saw so many people who themselves had been healed and trained, and who were now ministering to others. It was a miracle. Tears came as the grace of God began to unfold amongst the people. This was France, the country that Peter Horrobin, director and founder of Ellel Ministries, had called the toughest country he had experienced.

We worked very hard. I was both teaching and part of the prayer ministry team. In addition to the main sessions, people came to us for ministry on an appointment basis, up in the small flat above the conference centre, where we stayed whilst in France. Helen did all the listening, translating and summarising for me as we sought to understand and address the presenting problems and, having by now received much of the teaching herself, she was also roped in on occasions to pray with other delegates attending the conferences. We were a good team, and it has to be said that without Helen I would not have been able to do any prayer ministry.

Teaching lasted a long time because of the translation, but I found the interval between speaking and the translation gave me time to collect my thoughts.

God gave us strength. One evening, having already taught twice during the day, I was exhausted, but waiting to teach another session. Walking across from our flat to the church, I found myself crying out to God: "O God, have I still got your anointing for this next session?" The answer in my spirit was so clear – "Yes." It was so humbling.

Another enormous privilege we had was the unexpected opportunity to minister to French Jews. A number of these were beginning to rediscover their Jewish roots, having been born into families where many years of fear during the Second World War had led them to conceal their Jewish identity. Family members had been sent to concentration camps and killed, betrayed by their own countrymen. Now they were experiencing both the joy and the grief of this new realisation. We found ourselves encountering some of the deepest grief we had ever experienced, as we listened to their stories, but what a joy and privilege it was to support and pray with them, as they released their pain and anguish to God, and forgave those who had so wronged them and their families, finding a new peace.

We learnt so much during these months, but eventually it was time to come home. It was very sad to say goodbye.

A very big reason why I loved our time in France was that I found such freedom working alongside Patrick and helping him there as much as I could. Rather as in Acts, this was a new, emerging church with lots of problems and some clear demonic attacks – a bit raw at times, but so very real and very rewarding.

As far as I know at the time of writing, Ellel now has three centres in France. How exciting it has been to look on the internet and learn of the many live churches springing up all over France. Just to have been a very little part of that is humbling.

The time came when the journey from Plymouth to East Sussex was beginning to be too much. We had to make a decision to stay in Plymouth and cease involvement with Ellel or move to the south east. Well that's now history and we must have made one of the quickest house sales possible: I had set off for another weekend at Glyndley, but barely had I arrived when Helen called to say she had a firm buyer for the house, and it hadn't even been placed on the market! Our lovely home sold in a matter of days and we embarked on the next phase of adventure with God, staying initially in one of the Glyndley Manor cottages on site.

Our stay in the cottages lasted three months, followed by four years in a flat within the boundaries of the Cooden Beach Golf Club, before finding a more permanent home, where we have now been for over twelve years. That in itself would once again be a story of God's provision and timing which affected and blessed others, as well as us, but would take another full chapter to tell.

But times change. I was working very hard with Ellel and becoming tired and a little jaded. Many of the older folk had already retired, a few had gone to be with the Lord, and I began to realise I had been neglecting my wife. Circumstances demanded I take a fresh look at what I was doing and, sadly, I came to the decision that it was time for me to leave. How can you leave Ellel? I believe Paul talks about being 'poured out'. The understanding of that began to ring bells. Once again, I made my way down the long drive from Glyndley Manor, this time to close a chapter of my life which had been life changing. It had been a huge blessing and I was a changed person.

With Ellel Ministries I had been to India, France, Australia and Switzerland, not forgetting Scotland. They now embrace over 30 nations, even as far as China. It's now ten years since I left and, at eight-six, I still miss teaching, to be in that very special conference room, sharing the many-faceted gospel, seeing people's lives change, and being a part of the team. Yes, church is good, but not the same. However, God is good and ever faithful.

As this age seems to be drawing rapidly to a close, I'd like to dedicate this testimony to my wife Helen and my two children, Richard and Nicola, and to all those who from very early days have had some input into my life.

Those words from the elderly deacon at Muswell Hill Baptist Church ring in my mind: "You will be very disappointed in yourself but don't give up."

Those words, written by my dad in the Bible when I was born, Proverbs 7:1-2, still grip my heart: 'My son, keep my words and store up my commands within you. Keep my commands and you will live.'

His Word, His law, His statutes and, O yes, His grace! The closing verses of Romans 5 come to mind: 'Where sin increased, grace abounded all the more!' (New American Standard Bible)

Which leaves me simply to finish this account and to ask: 'Could I have made it without knowing Jesus? Not a chance!'

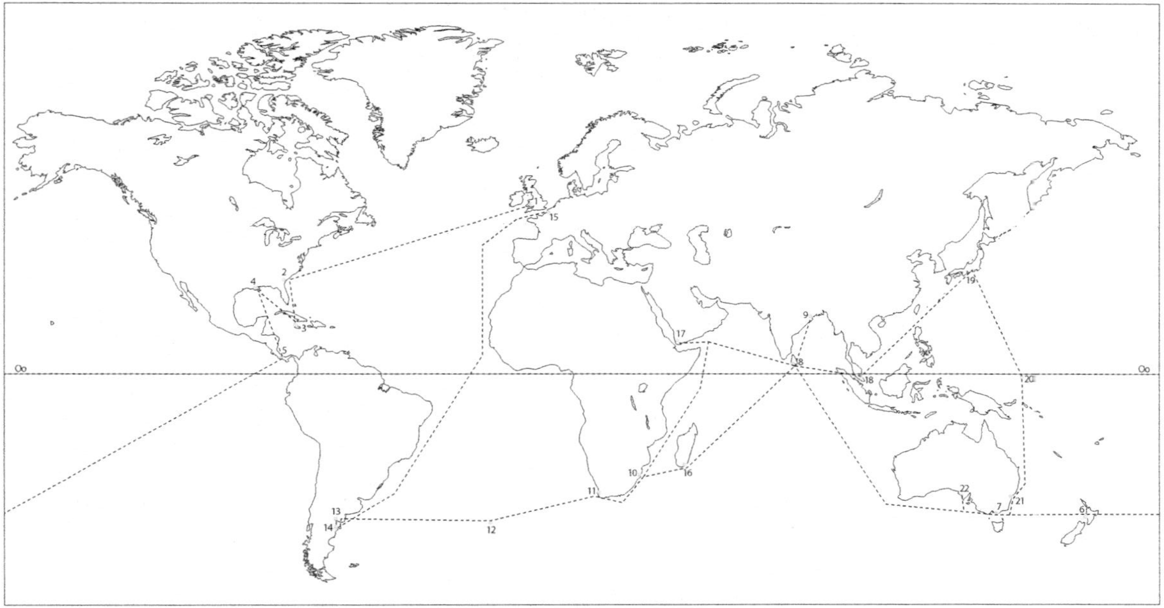

1.Cardiff
2. Newport News
3. Port Royal
4. New Orleans
5. Panama
6. New Plymouth
7. Melbourne/Geelong
8. Colombo
9. Calcutta
10. Durban
11. Capetown
12. Tristan Da Cunha
13. Montevideo
14. Buenos Aires
15. Antwerp
16.Durban
17. Aden
18. Singapore
19. Osaka
20. Nauru
21. Nevicastle
22. Ceduna

Voyages by Sheilbank (17 months) and Titanbank (27 months)
Included many return trips between India/Australia Australia/Nauru

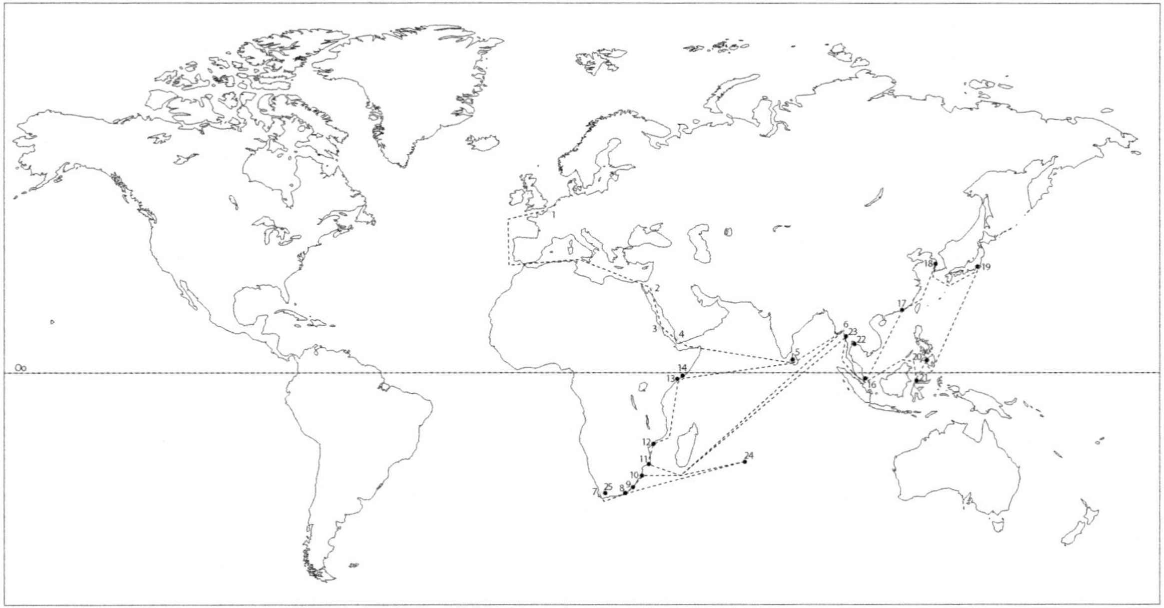

Voyage by Dartbank (grey dot)
Voyage by Ettrickbank (black dot) African Oriental Line

1. Zeebrugge
2. Suez
3. Port Sudan
4. Aden
5. Colombo
6. Chittagong
7. Capetown
8. Port Elizabeth
9. East London
10. Durban
11. Maputo (L.M)
12. Beira
13. Dar-Es-Salaam
14. Mombasa
15. Colombo
16. Singapore
17. Hong Kong
18. Inchon
19. Japan
20. Iloilo
21. Sandakan
22. Bangkok
23. Rangoon
24. Mauritius
25. Capetown

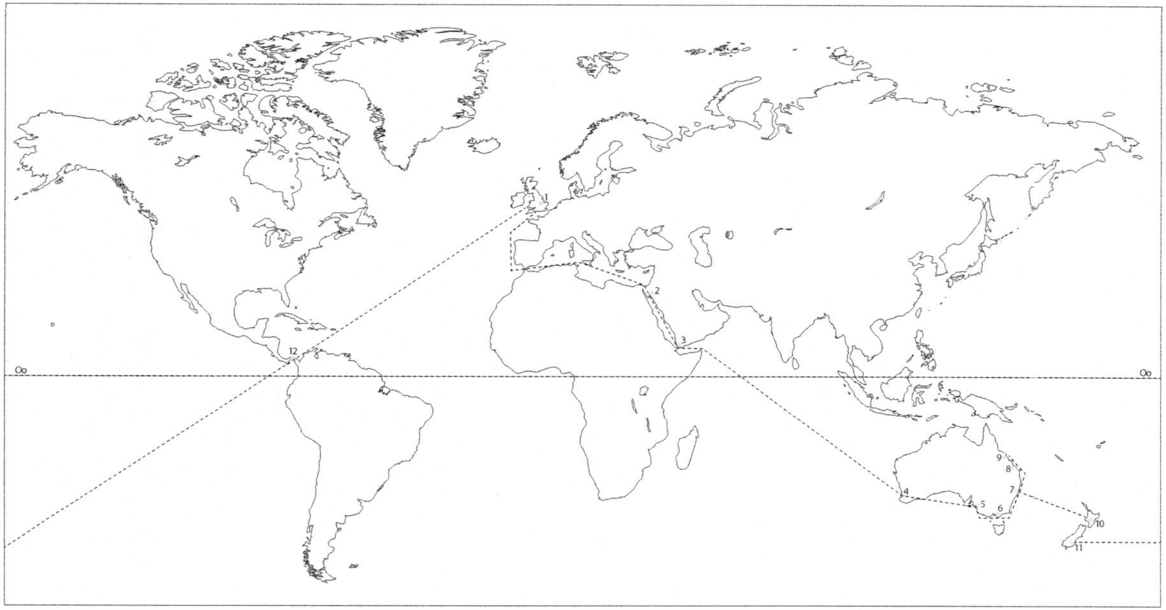

Shaw Savill Line. UK to Australia & New Zealand, via Suez & Panama Canal

1. UK Ports
London
Glasglow,
Liverpool
2. Suez
3. Aden
4. Freemantle
5. Adelaide
6. Melbourne
7. Sydney
8. Brisbane
9. Rockhampton
10. NZ North Island
Auckland
Bay of Island
Napier
Wellington
11. NZ South Island
Picton
Christchurch
Dunedin
Lyttleton

Glossary of Seagoing Terms

Azimuth mirror	=	mirror used to take compass bearings
Binnacle	=	casing in which a ship's compass is kept
Bulkheads	=	any vertical partitions separating one part of a ship from another, such as walls
Bulwarks	=	any side of the ship protruding above the decks
Bunkers	=	fuel stores
Bunkering	=	refuelling
Chippy	=	carpenter
Davits	=	devices for hoisting and lowering lifeboats
Derricks	=	booms for loading and unloading cargo
Fo'c'sle	=	forecastle, a short raised deck above the main deck at the front of the ship
Gunnies	=	large bales of hessian cloth
Hawsers	=	cables/large ropes used for tying ships to quayside
Liberty boat	=	the boat that takes sailors ashore
Monkey island	=	a small deck above the wheelhouse accessed for navigational purposes
Sparks	=	radio officer
Wool dumps	=	big bales of wool

Printed in Great Britain
by Amazon

28248870R00086